EXECUTIVE COACHING

EXECUTIVE COACHING

A PRACTITIONER'S GUIDE TO CREATING EXCELLENCE

SUNIL UNNY GUPTAN

SAGE | Response Business Books

www.sagepublications.com

Los Angeles • London • New Delhi • Singapore • Washington DC

First published in 2012 by

SAGE Response
B1/I-1 Mohan Cooperative Industrial Area
Mathura Road, New Delhi 110 044, India

SAGE Publications Inc
2455 Teller Road
Thousand Oaks, California 91320, USA

SAGE Publications Ltd
1 Oliver's Yard, 55 City Road
London EC1Y 1SP, United Kingdom

SAGE Publications Asia-Pacific Pte Ltd
33 Pekin Street
#02-01 Far East Square
Singapore 048763

Published by Vivek Mehra for SAGE Publications India Pvt Ltd, typeset in 10/12 pt Palatino Linotype by Diligent Typesetter, Delhi and printed at Chaman Enterprises, New Delhi.

Library of Congress Cataloging-in-Publication Data Available

ISBN: 978-81-321-0717-0 (PB)

The SAGE Team: Rekha Natarajan, Anupam Choudhury and Nand Kumar Jha

For Ishita

Impossible is an invitation

Thank you for choosing a SAGE product! If you have any comment, observation or feedback, I would like to personally hear from you. Please write to me at <u>contactceo@sagepub.in</u>

—Vivek Mehra, Managing Director and CEO,
SAGE Publications India Pvt Ltd, New Delhi

Bulk Sales

SAGE India offers special discounts for purchase of books in bulk. We also make available special imprints and excerpts from our books on demand.

For orders and enquiries, write to us at

Marketing Department
SAGE Publications India Pvt Ltd
B1/I-1, Mohan Cooperative Industrial Area
Mathura Road, Post Bag 7
New Delhi 110044, India
E-mail us at <u>marketing@sagepub.in</u>

Get to know more about SAGE, be invited to SAGE events, get on our mailing list. Write today to <u>marketing@sagepub.in</u>

This book is also available as an e-book.

CONTENTS

LIST OF CASELETS

PREFACE

TRAVEL WITH TIME or time passes you by. The gentle breeze you may hardly heed, or the gale-force gust that jerks you awake, may be the jet stream announcing that time has just sped past you. The speed may vary depending on your own relative momentum, but the fact is clear: *Time has overtaken you.*

But then it is all so much possible that you can stay a step or a mile ahead of time. The return on the effort put into staying ahead rides on the circumstances and the direction you are invested in.

And then there are also individuals of a rare breed amongst us who revel in the thrills of speed, in beating a competitive and equally fleet-footed time. For them, there just isn't anything called 'beyond reach'. They would have ripped the page that carried the word 'impossible' off the dictionary. For them, *impossible is an invitation.* An invitation to excel, an invitation to experience, an invitation to experiment and live life in full, as Tennyson's *Ulysses* says, '…drink life to the lees….'

This is one level of striving. And then, there are also those in running who help others run. The skill of the warrior is, in part, the skill of the charioteer. The genius of player in the field is often the craft of the coach working along the sidelines. The racer in his brilliance is the frontman for the trainer and the team working in the pit. The actor on screen is as outstanding as the director behind the scene. The bird that soars in majestic glory has the wind beneath its wings.

To be the person out there is one thing; having lived the road, leading others along the path and seeing them zip their way ahead revving their fine-tuned engines of courage is quite another high. The lead technician in the pit has as much the life of achievement in his craft as the Formula 1 driver popping champagne on the podium. Not quite in the arc light, life has as much or much more to offer and to be gained from. For them too, the challenge is in the invitation—the invitation to the seemingly impossible.

Some lives are incomplete without challenges. Some lives are left unlived unless driven by the quest for achievements placed at a stretch out of immediate reach. So much I have gained in seeing them at close quarters, navigating and seeking to strike bearing in such lives. Two decades I have spent in the dug-outs, pit stops and practice nets of the corporate fields and organizational playgrounds. Watching from the sidelines in the high-stake, high-stress games played out in corporate boardrooms, corner offices, cubicles and shop floors, I have witnessed a vast array of manoeuvres and mechanizations, played deliberately and in innocence. Handholding people in their journey out of the lonely depths of emotional misery in their personal lives, while also celebrating their ascent to soaring heights in public and professional fronts, has been in itself a gratifying reward.

Such has been my labour and life as an executive coach and mentor to several people in varying fields of work. People from different walks of organizational and public lives—CEOs, political executives, trade union leaders, social workers, school teachers, persons in sports, medical professionals, armed forces professionals, hoteliers, etc., have shared their lives and their hopes and travails with me. In the boardrooms and the marketplace, in government secretariats and in high-security laboratories, in dusty villages and in luxury resorts, have I had the joy of travelling in life with people who have sought to make themselves far better than they have been.

To these people I am in debt for much of my understanding and learning of the process and practice. I have grown because they have let me grow with them. This work is a tribute to their courage and conviction that life can always be made better with effort and striving. They can always work to becoming the best version of themselves in every instance of their lives.

The book cites real instances of real people and their labour, their triumphs and their ordeals. For reason of concern for their privacy and ethical commitment to confidentiality, the cases cited here have been masked with altered names, places and other obvious identifiers. Also, fictional techniques have been used in the narrative to enhance readability. As in any case study, redundant information and issues have been sheared to achieve focus on the issues and context of discussion. Life on the other hand comes packaged with clutter and the sometimes-confusing swath of inanities. The unisex 'he' is used here to denote both genders. Wherever gender itself is an issue, 'she', 'he' or 'she/he' is used. In other places, 'he' could be taken to mean 'she' as well.

In the making of this book, so much I owe to my wife and companion for over two decades, Surekha, for her patience with my preoccupations. Time and space spent on this effort have been those pilfered from what would otherwise have been hers. She has also been a part of the work in contributing so deep an understanding of people and relationships arising from her practice as a psychotherapist. Surely this work would have not seen the light nor made it through the tunnel without her help in staying the course.

My thanks go to those many other unsung folks and heroes who have shaped me to what I am today. So much has their contribution been in shaping my craft and capability. Some of them have become a part of this work, and all of them are my friends for life. These friends have all been as much a family to me as my family members have been my friends.

Several organizations have treated me as a part of themselves without my formally having to be on their rolls. They have been liberal in their affection towards me and have welcomed my work with their people over the years. I would particularly like to appreciate the efforts in Executive Coaching of Dr Reddy's Laboratories, Kenexa Technologies, Fresenius Kabi Oncology (India), Progress Software India and Matrix Laboratories.

Beyond the documentation of experience and practice is the need to garner resources and understanding of work along similar lines. I owe to my close friend and valued well-wisher, Dr Vidya Mani gratitude in being there and helping seek, source and access resources which have added depth to this work.

And then, there is Ishita...so young, and yet so much to feel old for...striving to not let chronological age catch up with other aspects of her. It has been my wealth and fortune to have been a part of such a life.

All of 19 years and a life brimming with accomplishments, she would, to herself, be an impossible benchmark, were she to live life all over again. In sport, in art, in music, in academics, among nerds and geeks or in the cool world, she can hold her own, on or within a whiff of the summit. Tireless energy to scheme and to navigate past any barrier that holds the restlessness at bay has been her calling card. She has ventured into worlds which to a young mind would have been very strange and alien, and yet emerged richer for the experience and the wisdom garnered.

This work is dedicated to her... To my daughter, Ishita. To celebrate the impossible. To celebrate the invitation. Not in quixotic quest, but with deliberate design—the hunger to know, the passion to experience and the desire to grow... *Impossible is an invitation.*

1. WHAT EXECUTIVE COACHING IS ALL ABOUT

In a perfect world, we would all be coaches...

ALMOST ALL OF us play the game as we see fit. We cheer small successes and chase the prospect of big achievements. There are a few of us who succeed big time and effectually become icons for others to look up to and try to emulate. Some others are content with lesser accomplishment and further down the line are those still labouring on with hope bravely flickering in their hearts.

Whichever the cluster each finds himself in, he sure would have advanced further had he the benefit of someone to hold forth the torch to light his way forward and show him the paths he alone may have been unable to see. We could do well with that kind of a torch bearer. Someone who not just lights up the path ahead or the scene around, but also helps find pathways within as well — pathways as yet unknown.

The journey, in career as in life, is not lived in the journey alone. There are greater achievements to be had in reaching further, faster and higher. While each of us has his own pace, often set by himself, there are also hidden sources of strength, energy, verve and even frolic that may never be known, were it not for someone skilled in unearthing and uncovering them to help us out.

So, who is this near magical person who comes equipped with the miraculous ability to see what we don't, to sense what we don't feel and perceive what is not apparent to us? Well, for one, the person himself would not appreciate being called magical or anything close to it. He would just like to see it as a professional would see himself: being good at what he does.

The executive coach gives people a makeover—of work performance, of job effectiveness, of career direction or of life. People critical to the organization's scheme of things; people seeking to get more out of their careers, jobs and life; people poised to take the leap into the next higher orbit; people morphing into new positions, functions and roles; people toiling under burdens of challenges, conflicts and contradictions; people seeking to make new moves in some aspects of their life; or people who live for challenging the wisdom of the possible and stretch beyond the known limits; these are people looking for association with someone who can help navigate the maze and make it with élan. The executive coach is the person being sought. He is in the race to help others win. In their winning is his victory.

Coaching is not a new enterprise. It has been around as long as people have had the need to find someone who will work with them exclusively and help them configure their success. The coach may not have come through the ages with the nomenclature, but the function is not at all new. But what seems novel is the adaptation of the approach to the field of organizations and management. The executive coach has moved silently into the inner corridors of the top floor and has sat comfortably amidst the mandarins of the boardroom. Just as much with ease, the coach has worked well with the people manning the lower branches of the organization or labouring in the workplaces of the shop floor.

Caselet 1 Astride the Winds of Change

The deal had been struck and inked. The massive changes expected were rolling in faster than anybody had expected. So much of the positive winds were blowing and the cobwebs of old practices were being blown away and even the old corners of the organization were being dusted clean. The shining new image of the merged larger organization was coming through so well. It was all going almost exactly to plan. We were, till the other day, two medium-sized companies not unknown, but not well-known either. With the merger deal working out, we are catapulted to the top of the league. And we are, today, in line to go global in operations. We are suddenly the big fish in the water.

With so much change sweeping across, there was the need to have someone to front it to the outside world—a world seeking to find out and come to terms with the new entity. On one hand there were these enormous pressures of work as the new Chief Executive Officer (CEO) and Vice-chairman in the new restructured set-up. On the other was the need to help people and the systems to adapt amicably and well with the change worked out. To add to this was the need to handle the external world.

I have never done this before; at least not at this scale. The string of invitation to address the top people from the Chamber of Commerce, the high-profile international visitors, the top government officials, the central and state ministers, the list was getting endless. The most difficult was the constant requests to be interviewed and spoken to by the emerging media. I just didn't know how I could get to know what and how to do all these. Pre-merger, we were a medium-sized company and we had our share of highs, but this was at a different scale altogether.

I had managed pretty well till now and I know I was successful and good at it. I could handle people well at all levels. I could communicate well enough. But why wasn't it falling in place? All that I tried was not going through at all. People just didn't understand or get what I was trying to do. Somehow, I didn't feel myself making the league of the big players and didn't seem to be able to be at ease in handling the big league and the big players. And then, I was getting stressed out.

Who could help me shape up to the new communication and role demands? Who do I trust to help me manage my image and training me to manage it myself? How could I get to be savvy at handling the media? How could I be effective in even speaking to the students at the top business schools? I really thought I needed an executive coach. He could be the one.

That was six months ago. Three months of work with my executive coach and today, I'm comfortable and so much at ease in all communication situations. I actually enjoy being interviewed on television, meeting with the big league and even the popularity I have with the top business school folks. I do look back and wonder how I could have been so out of my depth earlier in such simple matters. I really wonder why I did not enlist an executive coach earlier.

Coaches in the field of battle and warfare have long existed. They have trained and prepared warriors for combat and war. There have also been coaches in the area of statecraft and governance. They have worked with rulers, governors and administrators at the very top, getting them to be better at their rule and control. There have been mentors through the ages, handholding princes and kings in their quest for better governance and greatness. The field of sport gave rise to coaches in their own drive to get the athletes to become 'swifter, higher, stronger'. It is from sport that coaching came into the modern corporate offices.

Therefore, the model is more akin to the ones adopted in sport with developments and customization to suit the requirements of the modern corporate citizens. In sport, the coach is seen as someone who had played the game before with a measure of success and has an expertise in it. He is expected to transfer the knowledge and proficiency to the trainee athletes and increase their capabilities and performance as a mandate. In organizational context of coaching, however, the coach is seen as someone who has the competency and capability to help the employees in their learning and development efforts to enhance their performance on the job. Further on, the variety of applications of the coaching interventions has created their own niche for specialists in different forms and areas of coaching.

FROM TRICKLE TO TORRENT

Marshall Goldsmith set off the precursor to what eventually became executive coaching in the corporate context in organizations. His work in the areas of 360-degree feedback and leadership development evolved into the corporate executive coaching practices of today. Warren Bennis, Paul Hershey and others have significantly contributed in crafting coaching as a significant people-development practice in organizations. Timothy Gallwey carried coaching from the field of sport into organizations, taking off from his experience in coaching in tennis and other sport. His *Inner Game* series have been significant contributions to the field.

Even as late as the 1980s, there was little need felt for any form of specialized coaching in the organizations—even in the West. The Human Resources (HR) department was the purveyor of specific effort in the few cases that may have been seen to require an individualized intervention. This too was more remedial in nature than any pre-emptive attempt at learning and development. These sporadic forays by HR did not have any concerted plan, focus or theoretical framework to be guided by.

But then, even if late, the changes in the business and social environment brought about pressures to do better than what was the resident practices. The challenges forced the search for more effective developmental interventions to meet the pressures to establish excellence as the primary criterion for success in organizations. Some of the contributing factors snowballed into the intensity of the move forward to evolve better and more effective learning and development interventions for the critical people manning the upper reaches of the hierarchy.

The formal hierarchy began loosening up with better resources being available through non-traditional routes of growth within organizations. The need for diversity and openness to let expressions of views to foster innovations and exponential possibilities meant that merit be accorded higher status than was hitherto considered. The traditional bastions of power, confidence and influence began to open itself to more people who could offer higher and better contributions to managing and leading the organizations.

The long-held faith in age and seniority gave way to demonstrated merit and contribution to the organization. Human Resources, on its part, began the drive to seek greater investment into employee development plans and initiatives. Remedial development moved aside to accommodate ventures into learning and development as a strategic investment. The top team got greater share of focus in their need for inputs and help in the development initiatives. Coaching that was waiting in the wings began to move to the centre stage as the intervention of choice. From few and sporadic instances of application, coaching began as a widespread learning and development intervention in organizations.

COACHING IS A DIFFERENT DISCIPLINE

Coaching also differentiates itself from the therapeutic and counselling disciplines in that it has a clear focus on the issues and outcome of the intervention. They have to be significant for demonstrable indication of enhancement of present performance and aims to contribute to the betterment in foreseeable future.

There are a variety of areas and forms of coaching as a learning and development intervention. The common feature among all is that coaching is largely facilitative in style and nature, with the coach working to help the coachee learn from their own resource. However, there could also be times when the coach finds that the coachee is very ill-equipped in the learning process or is unfamiliar with or inexperienced in the area being worked upon. Here, the coach may have to provide the learning input and resource along with knowledge, illustration or explanation as a foundation to build the facilitation process later.

Coaching is also a process that works with individuals or with small groups of individuals. Coaches differentiate themselves from trainers and instructors in that the trainers and instructors teach people with inputs and directions to make them learn skills and knowledge, while the coach facilitates understanding, exploration, learning and practice. Coaching engagements are for a more focused and shorter duration than the mentoring association.

There are a variety of areas or specializations that coaching comes in in the organizational context. Each has a niche that it occupies and facilitates in assisting the coachee in the development effort. Choice of which coach is required would have to be worked out depending on the learning and development need of the coachee and the organizational need in making the investment in the intervention. Some of them overlap in their area of operation and work.

The business coach specializes in working within the organizational context of business and the strategies related to the conduct and furthering of the business of the organization. His focus is on the maximizing of the benefits of enhanced and better conduct of business and organizational processes and therefore works with the people to help in that direction. This form also overlaps considerably with the consulting process in organizational settings.

The other forms of coaching largely work with people more directly. They are often one-on-one and customized to individual requirements. The skill and performance coach, life coach, leadership coach, career coach, peer coach or buddy, etc., are examples of the different forms of coaching focused on to specific learning and development needs felt.

The executive coach is one working with the people in the higher levels of the organization—in executive positions in the hierarchy. These executives are key and critical people in the organizational scheme of things. They have characteristic needs of their own, with limitations that also accompany their position. The people in these positions have severe limitation of available time resources, often under pressure and stress of the responsibilities and accountability that go with their roles. They have high deliverables and output expectations riding on them. Their every move has higher stakes, risk and value vested in them. They are high-value people to the organization and those whom the organization is investing in to succeed. They are often high-strung and come with idiosyncrasies setting them apart from the people in the rest of the organization. The executive coach has to work with this group of people on a one-on-one intervention, customized to each individual.

The executive coach has to have a wider array of specialization, focus, tools and outlook than the other coaches in the field. They work with higher levels of credibility, capability, verve and alertness to match that of their coachees.

WHY HAVE AN EXECUTIVE COACH?

The executive coach is a trusted friend, a wise counsel and a teacher of sorts without the burden of being a mentor. From emperors and kings of yore to the CEOs and Heads of State of today, the need for having someone who can be relied upon to help imbibe the necessary capabilities, competencies and skills, ensure that that the right moves get taken and the slips guarded against, trusted to keep the confidence and provide the right advice and not having to look over the shoulder all the time and be sure to have the depth of wisdom has always been felt. There have been coaches that the best of people have taken on to make even that little or subtle bit of difference between being good and being great. The executive coach never competes against the coachee but is always there in every competition—alongside the coachee to help him emerge victorious.

The executive coach helps in making the growth into the next higher orbit in job, career or life easier to work towards. Transitions are never easy and having someone to walk you through the process makes it easier to navigate. The executive coach is someone who certainly has a better idea of the trails and pathways unfamiliar to the individual. Then again, facilitating the learning process of working through the transition prepares the individual to face similar and even higher challenges in the changed environment.

The executive coach is a willing and patient listener. It is fundamental to his job to be able to do this. Being so, the executive coach is a great asset as a sounding board to pretest the soundness of ideas before working them out to implementation or announcement. He also is an excellent instrument of catharsis in times of high stress and pressure of work or other emotive issues festering in the mind and eroding inner peace. Unburdening the restive contents within the safety of the trusted relationship makes way for greater clarity of thought.

Shedding the baggage of the past and working towards a make-over of work style and lifestyle needs someone to handhold and give the confidence that the moves are in the right direction and for the better. The executive coach is best placed to work with in this effort, especially when the stakes are high and risk of inappropriate changes are present. The counsel of the executive coach helps to see the proposed makeover in the right perspective and evaluate it for what it is actually worth before making the moves towards it.

The bane of being on the route to success is being pursued by issues and concerns—each more intricate, irritating and persistent than the previous one. They descend in a clutter, cutting out possible chance of rendering some sort of order in the way they may be approached. This is where some support from one who can understand them helps in clarifying and prioritizing them for what they are worth. The executive coach is the one needed when the situation, at times, appears claustrophobic. The executive coach works with the coachee to prioritize issues and concerns to resolve and work them out of the way.

Roles and positions in any organization or career—or for that matter, life itself—are a kind of unending sequence of transitions from one state of being to the next. Each state could be as radically different from the coming state as could possibly be. This puts the burden of making through the transition on the one making it. Here too, the executive coach is the one to seek help from in making the crossing that much ache- and pain-free.

Then again, for those on the heady high road to success often have the tough task of finding an equitable balance among different aspect of their life. While the professional facet gleams with the sheen of achievements, the downside of sacrificed personal or social life does not appear good at all. Finding the right balance can be quite a tough challenge. Figuring out the best combination and then working through it is sure a difficult task for someone already hard up for mindspace and time. Would it not be so good to have someone to advice or even suggest ways to be able to pack all of it into one life? Seek an executive coach!

The primary role of the executive coach is to be able to walk the coachee to enhance and effectually multiply safely the successes he has logged. This entails a series of moves which would work ways to widen the repertoire of capabilities and skills the coachee possesses. Honing and fine-tuning the skills and competencies, acquiring new ones, extending the range of existing ones, awakening dormant ones and making all of these more productive and active is what the executive coach can help the coachee achieve. The coach works with the coachee in figuring out the blind spot and working to get over it in the best possible way.

Exploring new directions of thought and activity, new directions in profession and careers, new and innovative means of seeking to make work and life more productive is what the executive coach can work with the coachee on in the process. While the explorations may take the coachee and the coach in directions and areas far afield, the coach also makes sure that the core issues and matters of concern are not compromised or let adrift. Getting these settled and worked out are at the heart of the Executive Coaching process. In the process, the coachee gets to experience and acquire the capability to stretch the horizon and the frame of reference that he could operate within. Divine and discover new sources of energy and verve to make that much of difference in output and achievement are opportunities that can open out to the coachee.

One of the essential needs for assuring success in the long term is to have clarity of the goals being targeted. Then again, whether the goals are realistic, whether they are too much of a stretch or whether one is underestimating one's capability of achievement can really be gauged when there is an unbiased observer to give any form of dispassionate feedback and analysis of the goals set. This essentially helps in recalibrating the goals as a more realistic challenge. Inviting the feedback and being able to identify and appreciate the unrecognized limitations and constraints is a good quality to imbibe. The executive coach's presence works well in providing these with ease.

Long-term association with an executive coach goes hand-in-hand with the ability to identify and reinforce the value set one would like to carry through life and in the professional settings. Recognizing values through debate and inquiry helps in being prepared to deal with issues in reality which question them. In the process, building a strong ethical outlook becomes a natural part of life.

The biggest benefit of having an executive coach stand by you in the game is to have him challenge and test ideas. The executive coach can be expected to be good at questioning assumptions of the coachee and help in validating them. That is basic to his job. The coach would also be one person who would not baulk at telling the coachee the truth as it is rather than pussyfoot around in deference to the status and stature of the coachee.

Navigating through the quagmire of the organizational dynamics would not be an easy affair unless one knows well the gullies and the alleyways. A guide there would be an asset even if he insists on playing with a straight bat. There is always the unexpected around the corner and predicting when another 'Doosra' will be bowled at the coachee is near impossible. Preparing the coachee in the best possible manner for the unpredictable nature of the organizational dynamics, and in life as well, is the brief the executive coach carries.

The coach could help the coachee find ways to build and maintain relationships at an even keel. Working to keep relationships— professional, social and personal—successful is often a high energy investment, but with great returns on it too. Keeping them stable and healthy is among the best investments that any senior executive could make.

Sometimes, the tough life of a senior executive does lead them into the need to make hard and unpleasant decisions. These decisions could cause devastating impact on the executive unless he has an outlet to catharsis and assuage the unwarranted feeling of guilt at times. Here, the executive coach can walk the coachee through the paces to work out the equitable way of perceiving the decision and choice that had to be made.

There are numerous gains and advantages to be garnered in working with an executive coach. Going through the process can make a huge difference in the value addition the coachee can bring in to himself and the better quality of life that would result.

WHAT COULD GO WRONG?

The Executive Coaching process is not all rosy and devoid of downside and darkness. There sure are shady and seamy sides to the process as well. Awareness of it is good and necessary to navigate past them to reach the fruits of the labour invested.

The intervention could go wrong at the very beginning if the initial steps are not taken to build the context and nature of the relationship. This leads inevitably to either of them feeling unable to work with the other as the required element of trust would fall short. Therefore, the relationship could be fractured and the process does not take off at all.

The investment of trust and confidentiality that are the cornerstones of the process are vital. Either of them being breached could leave both the coach and the coachee feeling betrayed and violated in the process. The hurt could run deep and the recovery could be painful too. The process of initiation into the intervention is best taken slowly and with care, particularly when the coachee is sensitive. The coach may also not be as experienced in handling different people with idiosyncrasy he is not familiar with.

If there is insufficient investment of interest or effort from either side, the process could slow down and halt, which could also affect adversely the confidence in the intervention. This often leads to the intervention being abandoned. The other reason that often comes in the way of success in the intervention is the lower priority that the process is accorded by the coachee in the scheme of things. The process being largely a coachee-centred one, the investment of interest and the 'push' has to mainly come from the coachee. The executive coach would not pressurize the coachee to stay in the intervention as any change that may be need to be tried out and internalized has to be worked with by the coachee himself.

The frightful part of the process is in the subversion of the information and confidence that the coachee shares with the coach. An unethical and unscrupulous coach can put the profession, the intervention and the entire community to shame with this form of serious indiscretion. Dreadful as the prospect is, caution in checking out the executive coach before entering into any form of relationship would be the best defence against such an occurrence.

There is also the issue and possibility of interference in the process, relationship and activity by HR or the organization. Any seasoned executive coach can see this coming and can head it off before it becomes any form of serious threat. But it does damage the credibility of the process and also adversely affects the confidence of the coachee.

WHO SHOULD READ THIS BOOK?

This book is for different people looking for different things in the process of Executive Coaching. It seeks to address the needs in many ways, not all in one set or pattern but in ways to quench the thirst and create an interest to delve further into the interesting process. It works to provide an opportunity to leverage being in the process to garner greater good from the investment made. For the practitioner, it aims to present deeper insights to help improve practice. It is also to share with the professional community some of the experiences logged in practice.

Difficult as it is to cover a wide swath, there are indicators on how and where to seek more for those interested in looking further and probing deeper than the book is able to deal with. The book also looks to address in interesting manner the needs of the well-informed as well as the lay reader in different parts and in different forms.

For the practitioner, there is the advantage of checking out and validating the practices being carried out. It is an opportunity to compare experiences and perspectives on issues in the practice of Executive Coaching. To take note of possible cautions and checks that may have been missed in the bustle of the practice, and to run through a checklist of good practices that would provide greater insights into success would certainly be good. The book also works at offering a confirmation of direction and help in widening the horizon with respect to the practice.

The practitioner could also seek to enlarge the repertoire of skills and acquire new ones to enhance effectiveness. There is new energy and faith to be had from knowing different ideas on the theme. In enhancing the effectiveness of the executive coach, there is much to be offered to the coachee.

Avoiding the stone someone else has tripped on, working past barriers others have experienced and being able to avoid pitfalls others have stumbled into would definitely make for a safer journey. The issues and concerns experienced by organizations do vary. Being in the know of how different organizations experience such interventions does contribute to preparedness.

There is much for the professionals in the HR departments who would be called to champion the intervention in the organization. The means to conceptualize, design and put into place a high value intervention of this kind would go a long way in heightening the standing and credibility of the department. The checklist of steps for working through the process makes for being correct in the approach and implementation. Knowing the cautions to be taken and symptoms of things going wrong would help catch difficulties before they become severe. The sensitive elements in the process such as evaluation, briefing the executive coaches, handling the coachees are areas to prepare for in advance with the knowledge of how they work. HR being critical to the success of the process in the organization, there is much for them to understand and work with.

For people new to the process, it does provide a good insight into what the world of Executive Coaching is all about. The beginner can get a glimpse into the apparent intricacies of the process, the seemingly mysterious person the executive coach appears to be initially, the role of others like the HR department and the top team in the organization do play in the process and the preparation that may be needed when one does decide to wade in.

WHAT'S IN THE BOOK?

The chapter following this walks the reader through the different popular approaches to the practice of Executive Coaching. The coach has a menu of approaches and theoretical frameworks to choose from, depending on the nature of the intervention, the coachee he is working with, the issue being worked upon at the time, the preferred style of the coach, etc. His choice would be to make the optimal decision in the best interest of taking the coachee forward and getting the best result in the process. There are several approaches that have been practiced by experts in the field of psychology, sociology, management sciences and related disciplines. While there is no one-size-fits-all approach, it is best to customize the approach to the needs of the intervention.

Chapter 2 is also a walking tour of the different genres of coaching that the executive coach may decide to adopt. The choice of genre would depend on what objectives are set for the intervention and how the best output can be obtained in the process. The chapter is laden with concepts and issues in psychology and other fields of study that have been the contributors to making coaching a rich practice. This does lend to making the chapter a trifle heavy in reading for a lay reader, although every attempt has been made to keep it shorn of jargon.

Executive Coaching process has certain stages and landmarks that help in understanding the progress in it. These are steps that work to know what the events and results in the process are expected to be and whether the direction is right too. They may not be linear and sequential in practice but understanding them does help in knowing where and at what stage one is. Chapter 3 looks at the Executive Coaching's process and structure.

For the new entrant and those choosing to enter as a coachee, it is good to walk in prepared for what needs to be done to get the best out of the effort and investment. The pre-intervention preparation and work to be done by the coachee that would add value to the process are discussed in Chapter 4.

Chapter 5 discusses the executive coach. It looks at the qualities that set this person apart from others in the learning and development profession, the competencies, capabilities and skills that are needed to work successfully as an executive coach. There is also the element of attitude, orientation and value base that make up the executive coach. Understanding these is important too.

The executive coach has a toolkit he carries in which there is a tool specifically crafted for each need he may have in the process. There is a wide repertoire available to him in the practice of his trade. Chapter 6 discusses the oft used and the popular ones. In introducing the tools, their evolution, their utility, the cautions, the output expected and the expertise required are mentioned. There is much to be learnt and understood about the coachee and the process from the information generated through using the tools.

Any human interaction, particularly the ones that looks at development and growth, can be expected to be laden with concerns and issues between the parties involved and also the system sponsoring it. So it is too with the Executive Coaching process. Chapter 7 discusses some of the contentious ones that often pose a threat to the fruitful continuation of the intervention. The precautions and care that need to be taken to ensure these issues do not fester and spread. Otherwise, they could contaminate the entire effort and crash the investment.

What could organizations do to create good and favourable substrata for the positive learning and development intervention to germinate and grow? The steps to build helpful Learning and Development (L&D) culture in the organization are dealt with in Chapter 8. The culture is built over time and with the inputs and efforts of several people in the organization. The principal stakeholders, the champions and the beneficiaries in the organization are the ones who can create a good Executive Coaching environment.

The process owner—and, in the end, the natural beneficiary—is after all the HR department. Being the basic custodian of the employee development process, the responsibility falls on HR to handhold the process till it is able to take off on its own. There are ways in which the HR department can ensure success in introducing and nurturing the Executive Coaching intervention in the organization. There is much to be gained from this initiative if handled well. The advisory on how HR can work to lead the intervention to fructification is discussed in Chapter 9.

Most of us have questions on all things concerning us. And we would like to have some quick answers that give us a to-the-point idea of what we seek without the burden of having to read or look through tomes. So we have Frequently Asked Questions (FAQs). Chapter 10 has FAQs on Executive Coaching, dealing with questions that are often asked with succinct answers too.

The book is designed to lead the reader into being interested in Executive Coaching and the dynamics that makes it work. There is always more that someone wanting to seek can work on depending on the direction of depth he seeks. Chapter 11 is a lead on to where someone can source additional material on the subject should he want to delve further and search for more detail. The 'Additional Reading' is meant to be exactly that—additional, and beyond what is contained here.

So, let's stride forth and journey into the world of Executive Coaching.

2. APPROACHES TO EXECUTIVE COACHING

EXECUTIVE COACHING COMES with the strong backing of coaching practices principally in the field of psychology. There are several approaches in this field which lends direction and directives to the choice of coaching practices. Over long years of refinement and carefully evaluated evolution, the approaches have acquired distinct differences in how to help the practitioner arrive at solutions and goals sort after. Executive Coaching has, in a sense, combined several approaches and genres of coaching effort. The strong foundations in the different approaches also help executive coaches work out the best methodology to follow in assisting the coachees get the most out of the being in the intervention.

There are several approaches that have evolved in the field. Some of the important ones that have contributed to making the practice of Executive Coaching what it is today are discussed here. Also discussed here are the genres of coaching that have come into being over the years of practice of coaching itself. These forms of coaching have different foci and methodology in practice distinct from one another. They contribute to enriching the repertoire of the executive coach in adopting one which suits the coachee and the context. The familiarity, understanding and also expertise of the executive coach with the different approaches and genres equip him with the ability to choose and also navigate between them when needed.

The discussions here are not intended to be a study of the approach and genres themselves but an indicative description of each that influence Executive Coaching in its various forms today. First are the different approaches to coaching practices.

PSYCHODYNAMIC APPROACH

The Psychodynamic Approach is a highly influential technique and very vital in coaching. This has been in the forefront of coaching approaches at the very start of the practice. Most coaching in some form is drawn from the Psychodynamic Approach.

The Psychodynamic Approach is a body of work that concerns itself with the working of the human mind. It has grown in stature and depth over the past century from the Freudian concept of psychoanalysis to several clusters of models and theories that support the understanding of connectivity of the human mind to behaviour and the intricate synapses that hold it in place.

With regard to coaching, its primary role has been to link different forms of behaviour and behavioural modifications during the process to the understanding of the drive arising from the unconscious and the conscious mind of the coachee. It also tries to seek linkage to different parts of the mind and their functioning. In the process to seek to understand, clarify and, if necessary, correct the behavioural aspects of the coachee's functioning.

The ardent followers of using this approach in coaching emphasize the need to look at the individual not as an independent entity, but as a part of the organizational system. The organizational system influences the psyche and the behaviour of the individual contributing to the makeup of their personality as much as the individual influences the dynamics of the system within the organization. The Organizational Role Consulting Methodology, developed at the Tavistock Institute from the 1960s, applying this systems outlook to the Psychodynamic Approach is often considered a precursor to Executive Coaching as an organizational tool of individual development.

Understanding the working of the Psychodynamic Approach and its application equips the coach with the ability to deal with different aspects of the coachee's behaviour, get a holistic picture of the functioning of his mind and look at possible issues and resolution of them thereof. It also helps in getting the coach to work at building what is often called a safe 'holding environment' for the coachee and the relationship in coaching to work in.

The 'holding environment' is what the famed psychoanalyst Donald Winnicott described as a space within which the transactions and relationships can be built with the feeling of safety for the participants. This has been a crucial addition in the approach to psychotherapy since it was first described in the early part of the last century.

The 'holding environment', though not as much in the tradition of psychotherapy, in coaching has been a critical addition as well. In so far as the application of the concept is concerned, the creation of the 'safe environment' within which the coach and the coachee can interact and function in the context of the relationship, has been critical to the coaching process itself. Most coaches, either with deliberate planning and design or by instinctual feel, have worked to create a 'holding environment' in the coaching process.

The coach, in most cases, seeks to understand and work with the coachee's unconscious patterns of behaviour in many ways. The Psychodynamic Approach, in its various forms, contributes to the development of approaches and techniques to augment and add value to the process. While not going into the depths of the psychodynamic approaches, unlike counselling or psychotherapy, coaches use some of the techniques and approaches to derive the benefits of it without getting bogged down in the details of the concept and the rigors of the psychodynamic system.

Further down from the relative 'safety' of the 'holding environment' created using techniques and approaches in the psychodynamics, coaching also draws upon it to understand and work with the coachees. At times the coach may use it to overcome the defence mechanisms and self-protecting psychological strategies of the coachees in dealing with issues and matters that cause distress or anxiety.

The Psychodynamic Approach in coaching also highlights the use of techniques in dealing with transference and countertransference during the process of coaching. Understanding the dynamic in the process helps the coach use them in the process to gain access to and get a deeper understanding of the working of the coachee's mind in the process. It also works to weld a closer and more trusting relationship in the process in understanding the impact the coachee has on the coach himself. This could be in terms of the reactive processes that are evoked in them during the process of coaching intervention and interaction.

The coach well-versed in the approaches can gain deeper and more meaningful insights into the past and present thinking and understanding, and working of the mind of the coachee. Thus, in creating a linkage between the past and the present, identification of the issues to be dealt with, the solutions to be found and, finally, the advantages to be garnered by the coachee in the process can be worked out.

Different context of coaching are used in the Psychodynamic Approach to differing degrees and in different forms, so to say. Development coaching is often the greatest beneficiary of the use of this approach. To varying degrees, transformational, leadership and life coaching uses the techniques of the Psychodynamic Approaches as well. To a much lesser degree is the coaching that focuses on skill and performance coaching, career and peer coaching.

The Psychodynamic Approach in Executive Coaching has tremendous advantages in creating an open mind, in creating a stronger and deeper understanding of self and others in the coachee. It helps the executive coach understand the depth of the actions and rationalize the actions of the coachee. It works well in creating a good and firm understanding strategy of managing relationships and boundaries between people through understanding the action and behaviour of people. This becomes all so critical in leadership and leadership development.

At the same time, it must also be said that the use of the approach has some limitations in its applicability in the Executive Coaching process. The depth of the engagement required in the approach is rather inappropriate at times for the purposes of Executive Coaching. Applying the approach in coaching as a standard would leave the coaches often feeling unqualified and inadequate in the working of the process. Coaching often looks at being involved in a short engagement while the increasing involvement in the process of Psychodynamic Approach calls for deeper and, most of the times, a longitudinal involvement. This may be counterproductive if it runs counter to the set objectives of the Executive Coaching process itself. Further, the Psychodynamic Approach at times is over-concerned with solution to 'problems' identified in the process itself. It also, at times, takes on a prescriptive tone that may not be conducive to the coaching approach.

Applied with understanding and clarity of the process, the Psychodynamic Approach contributes hugely to the successful functioning and outcome in the Executive Coaching process. But then the preparedness of the executive coach in using and rationally applying the approach is the critical factor.

COGNITIVE BEHAVIOURAL APPROACH

Cognitive behavioural coaching has been variably described as 'an integrative approach which combines the use of cognitive behavioural, emotional and problem-solving techniques and strategies within a cognitive behavioural framework to enable the coaches to achieve their realistic goals' (Palmer and Szymanaska, 2007 : 86 as quoted in Cox, Bachkirova and Clutterbuck, 2010: 37).

The 1990s saw the increasing use of the Cognitive Behavioural Approach in coaching, integrating series of work done in the field of cognitive behavioural therapy and the theoretical framework developed in the approach. They tried to work at a coaching approach that included theories developed in fields like cognitive behavioural, solution focused approach, the rational emotive behavioural, social cognitive theories. The grand design lead to different models of coaching evolved to include the best approaches and techniques to optimize the outcome in coaching.

The Cognitive Behavioural Approach has veered around the belief articulated by Neenan and Dryden (2002), 'the way you think about events profoundly affects the way you feel about them', which in turn affects stress and performance. Thus, working at the thinking part of the coachee has been the cornerstone in the approach. There is also the dominant awareness of the 'internal dialogue', as described by Aaron T. Beck in 1976 and further worked on by others, in the approach. The 'inner dialogue' is the critical inner voice swirling around inside the individuals' head affecting the self esteem and creating self-doubts and impacting self-efficiency, competence and self-worth.

The effort in the Cognitive Behavioural Approach is to convert negative 'automatic thoughts' into positive ones. Correcting the unhelpful cognitive schema that lead to negative thoughts and working to recognize 'intermediate and core beliefs' that are generally understood to have been scripted in early childhood is the effort. This follows what Judith Beck (1995) described as three levels of cognition—automatic thoughts, intermediate beliefs (attitudes, rules, assumptions) and core beliefs. Several forms of cognitive or thinking errors identified that are common faults in processing of thoughts.

The Cognitive Behavioural Approach works at helping the coachee understand the barriers that impede or retard progress towards achievement of goal, and therefore set realistic goals for self. The approach also significantly tries to clarify the thinking process and make behaviours more realistic to the environment, along with trying to build internal stability that helps individual become more self-reliant.

The heightened self-awareness and increased self-acceptance works well to help the individual be more effective in dealing with and developing better performance outputs. They also work at the thinking skills in terms of trying to modify stress-inducing thinking towards more productive capabilities in coping and resilience.

There have been several 'models' of coaching based on the Cognitive Behavioural Approach that have led coaching practices. The 2001 model on PITS and PETS put forward by Neenan and Palmer discusses converting 'performance interfering thoughts' (PITS) into 'performance enhancing thoughts' (PETS). The SPACE model is also significant in that it discussed a holistic approach. SPACE is an abbreviation for the elements discussed in the approach— Social context, Physical and psychological reach, Action/inaction, Cognition and Emotion.

There is the ABCDEF model (Ellis et al., 1997; Palmer, 2002 and 2009) based on the Ellis' ABC model of emotional disturbance. Here, A (an activating event or an awareness) is mediated by B (beliefs and perceptions) causing C (consequence—emotional, behavioural, physical). D in the model is about disrupting and reconsidering these beliefs to develop E (effective new approach or response which would be shift from the old one). F represents the future focus that is encouraged in dealing with the goals and objectives set at personal and performance levels.

Another significant model put forth by Professor Stephen Palmer (2002, 2008) is the PRACTICE model. This works on (P) roblem identification; developing (R)ealistic and relevant goals; (A)lternative solution generation; (C)onsideration of the consequences; (T)argeting the most feasible solutions; (I)mplementing the (C)hosen solutions; and (E)valuating and reviewing the process.

While there have been significant contributions and success in the adoption of the Cognitive Behavioural Approaches in coaching, it has not been a road unaffected by evaluative discussions and dissent in the use of the approach. There is also the strong need for the coach to be well-versed with the methodology and practices in the approach for the successes to be garnered, and the recognition of the hazards in applying the approach by people less qualified or unqualified in its use.

The method has a strong psychological basis of understanding the coachee. Therefore, the willingness of the coachee to be subject to this depth of analysis is essential for the adoption of the approach. The acceptance of the suggestions and the opinions of the coach by the coachee are critical in the adoption of the emerging solutions in the approach.

GESTALT APPROACH

The Gestalt therapy and approach in psychology was developed by Fritz Perls, Laura Perls and Paul Goodman in the 1940s and 1950s. It is an existential form of psychotherapy.

Gestalt focuses on the individual's or, for that matter, system's experiences in the present moment and the environmental context or 'field' in which it takes place. It also centres on the adjustments that the individual or system makes as a result of the interactions with the context and the overall situation. Here, so much rests on the individual and the system in their effort to relate to the present and find meaning in the interaction. The effort to understand oneself in the present and seek to work with the clarity that emerges helps in adopting necessary changes and adapting to them.

There are some primary assumptions and beliefs that Gestalt Approach works with. People make an effort to do the best they can under the circumstance. Change is possible when one is in conscious contact with the 'truth' of an experience in the present. This is preferable to trying to be different and even either not recognizing or disowning parts of themselves and their feeling. Greater awareness affords people the ability to sort, organize and plan new ways of awareness, thinking and also behaviour.

The assumptions carry further into believing that individual behaviours cannot be fully understood or appreciated without reference to the context in which it takes place. Exploring the experience in the immediate setting and time—here and now— creates new avenues for learning and growth. Energy and mind invested in blind-end and unfinished agenda drains motivation, dilutes focus and retards progress towards utilization of the full potential to seek new avenues and opportunities.

The Gestalt coach's approach would be to understand the coachee in terms of his ability to look at himself in the present moment and relate to the circumstances and issues arising out of his interactions 'here and now'. The coach helps the coachee relate in these terms and understand his own processes and behaviour patterns, and therefore plan changes for the better. There is a strong emphasis on the intentional use of the 'self' and the 'present' as an instrument of change.

The coach also stresses the importance of the coach–coachee relationship and what is called the 'authentic dialogue' that takes place. The coach and the coachee have to implicitly understand that both will undergo changes within themselves as a result of the association in the relationship and effort at arriving at positive changes in the coachee. While the coachee works at his own awareness, assimilation of learning and change, the coach too is not immune to possible change within.

The Gestalt Approach is powerful as an instrument and requires coaches well-versed in taking on the approach and following through to the logical conclusion of the effort and association. The coachee should also be made aware and understand the power of the process and the investments needed to work through the process. This is a popular approach often taken by those well into the Gestalt school of thinking and are convinced of the efficacy and ability to produce positive changes even in difficult circumstances.

PERSON-CENTRED APPROACH

The Person-centred Approach has its beginning in what Carl Rogers set off in the 1940s and 1950s as the client-centred approach to psychology and work in the field. It was then seen as an alternative approach to the dominant models of behaviouralism and psychoanalysis and the nascent humanistic psychology. These models and their approaches to efforts at counselling and dealing with mental health issues of the time had a wide acceptance in the fraternity. Carl Rogers' alternative was to look at the process from the other side.

The Client-centred or the Person-centred Approach puts the receiver at the centre of the process and looks at it from his perspective, giving him a greater role in the process itself. The Person-centred Approach works with the fundamental belief that the individual is best placed to grow and hear his own inner desires. They can become their own best experts if given the right conditions and assistance.

The coach using this approach works at creating the best possible environment within the context of the relationship of coaching that would facilitate the coachee actualize his own inner desires through understanding of the experiences. The coach facilitates the coachee's understanding the experiences in the right perspective without fearing his own interpretations taking over that of the coachee's in most situations.

The approach is largely non-directive and lets the process, and outcome, be guided more by the coachee. This is achieved by the coach placing an ethical value on the non-interference in the desires and the right to self-determination of the coachee. While this is not to say that the direction and the process is entirely controlled by the coachee but that the role of the coach is facilitative in helping the coachee indentify, understand and determine what would be best in his own interest. The operational issue here is the mutual understanding of what would be in the best interest of the coachee without imposition of the coach.

TRANSACTIONAL ANALYSIS APPROACH

The basic philosophy of Transactional Analysis (TA) of being individuals in a connected world influences the approach of coaching itself. The philosophy is of being in the world as individuals yet related to others in the world and having the aspirational ties of trust, respect and well-being or, otherwise, of each other. The state colloquially referred to as 'I'm OK, you're OK' is a sure guide to the TA approach to coaching.

The TA approach is generally shorn of jargon and is client-friendly. Eric Berne, the originator of TA, believed in simplified language giving greater access to client rather than clothing understanding in the precision-obsessed approaches of the psychoanalytic profession. Berne believed that intention, beliefs and decision can be inferred from observation by clients as well as the therapist, and also checked out. This forms the basis for change.

The TA-based approach aims at the primacy of the autonomy of the client and the ability to change based on the underlying philosophy. The base premise is in : (a) the belief and faith in the worth and dignity of all people; (b) the ability of each to think and find solutions and solve problems; and (c) everyone's ability to change and adopt change in their thinking, behaviour, feeling and beliefs voluntarily. Respecting the autonomy of the individual is encouraged to seek self-determination, independence or interdependence.

Exploring the client's conflict zones in the transactions made, the TA approach aims at understanding the underlying script and the propensity towards what the TA tradition calls games. This helps the individual garner a deeper and better understanding of self and the interfaces with the environment, and thus plan and prepare for changes where necessary.

The advocates and proponents of TA approach tend to interpret observations largely within the framework of TA, moving little to accommodate the variations or validations that other traditions and approaches may offer. While TA has seen a fair amount of success and following in the corporate L&D set-ups, the more orthodox psychotherapy fraternities do look askance at it.

ONTOLOGICAL APPROACH

Ontology is the study of being and of reality, in particular, the investigation into the nature of human existence. This approach requires the entities involved to be in touch with the understood nature of their own existence as a standpoint of relating with the others in the process.

The coach has the basic responsibility of managing his own notion of existence and being in the coaching context and interaction with the coachee. The approach believes in the coach operating from his own way of being which can acutely affect the observation of the coachee's specific way of being in the same context. In this way, they can influence and facilitate a shift in the coachee's notions of being.

The coach should create a safe and secure environment for enquiry, observation, listening to and discovering through respectful relationship with the coachee. The coach has to primarily respect the individual boundaries of the coachee.

In this approach, the centrality of language, emotions and the body as a whole is emphasized. Beyond the proficiency, the stress is on the acceptance of the relationships as integral entities in the process.

TRANSPERSONAL APPROACH

Transpersonal Approach to coaching is not one often visited. This is more to do with the reason of the basic philosophy not being accepted by many in the fraternity.

Transpersonal Approach believes in seeing the human mind as infinite and human soul as divine. The belief itself is something many clients find hard to understand, follow and live by. Transpersonal Approach believes in going beyond the obvious aspects of the physical being of the person and looking at the other dimensions to seek paths to go forward. They take human as spiritual beings with a soul and spirit.

Transpersonal is not extra-personal, not religious or spiritual in the conventional sense. It also does not lay claim to being 'new age' in the way it sees issues and concerns. There is the distinction drawn between the pre-personal, the personal and the transpersonal. The pre-personal is the time in the process of prenatal development and childhood, the personal dealing with everyday consciousness and being and the transpersonal goes beyond into the realm of the divine, sacred and the holy. This is often the cause of discomfort for most people.

In Transpersonal Approach, the coach plays the role of a wise fellow traveller and an unassuming companion. There is no authority or power issue; no attempt at being directive or critical; nor is there a concern of superiority, expertise or being a repository of all knowledge that comes in the way of the relationship. The association of the coach with the coachee is undemanding, sincere, authentic, forthright and continually offering different dimensions for consideration.

As the coach and the coachee traverse the different levels of learning and enquiry, the transformation of the coachee takes place. The bounds of the beliefs and long-held convictions that hinder or retard their progress towards higher and more profound achievements get loosened and a new understanding and facilitative acceptance emerges. There is no tangible task or goal set but growth and progress are mutually understood between the coach and the coachee.

This approach is akin to the 'internship' that the *shishya* undergoes with the spiritual *guru* in the Indian tradition.

These approaches presented here are some of the better known and significant ones that have impacted and moulded the approaches to Executive Coaching as we know it today. There are several others too that have also contributed in some form or small ways— like the Existential Approach, the Neuro-linguistic Programming Approach or the Cognitive Developmental Approach. These can also be looked into for the nuances and possible smaller details.

Coaching has also evolved in several genres in terms of the focus or the practice of it in the industrial or corporate context. Understanding these are important in seeing the different options available in adopting coaching and moving into Executive Coaching as an intervention of choice in the L&D interventions in the organization for the high value employees.

MANAGER AS COACH

One of the key things about being a good and effective manager in organizations is to believe that subordinate development is an integral part of the managerial responsibility. The relevance and requirement for the growth and eventually success of the organization is a non-negotiable proposition. The manager who begins looking at his work and role from this standpoint often finds himself being not only more effective but also more popular and being liked much within his sphere of influence.

Managers who have taken on the role of being effective coaches, either as a part of the role itself or as a transition into it, have a set of characteristics that go beyond the conventional definition of managers. They tend to have an attitude of helpfulness and the quality of 'otherness' about them. They have a good ability to empathize with others in their dealing. They look to the prospect to help others seek opportunities to move towards bettering themselves, not just in the performance of their jobs but also in the overall capabilities and competencies.

These are people with less need for control and projection of their own persona. The manager-coach tends to be more open to personal learning and receiving feedback. They operate from a set of high personal standards mostly without imposing them on others. While patience is available in adequate measure, they also are not tolerant of others not measuring up without sincere effort.

The coaching mindset includes propagating the belief that it is a part of the role itself. They believe in not only moving themselves but also helping others transition from the telling, judging, controlling, directing approach and definition of their work to helping, developing, empowering and supporting definition of their role in the organizational context.

Unlike a 'missionary-style' leader and manager, the coach does not compromise on the expectation of efficiency and effectiveness in task performance and output from his subordinates. He may choose authority to drive home a point, but would prefer to clothe it in developmental terms.

TEAM COACHING

Coaching in the context of team is not really new as the others in the organizational context. Team coaching has been practised in the field of sport well before the thought of it came into the organizational realm. Most team sport has a coach working almost full-time alongside all the rest of the team infrastructure and functionaries. However, unlike the sport team coaching, organizational team coaching differs widely as much due to the nature of the teams as the work, purpose and objectives of the teams.

While the team coaches abound in their availability to organizations today, they function more as team building trainers and behavioural facilitators than as team coaches as such. Team coaches are more implants in functioning teams than consultants or visitors to the process. This principal differentiation makes for the rest of variation between team coaches and L&D assistance partners for teams within organizations.

In team coaching as a genre, the approach itself depends upon the stage of development of the team and the specific characteristic of the team. There cannot be a one-size-fits-all outlook to the way in which team coaching works. While the output and productivity of the team will always remain the principal issue, the focus would shift depending on the stage in the development of the team. The early stages of team development would require the coach to be more focused on the mechanics of formation and integration of the team—moving them from functioning group to team. Later on, the focus would be on the development and consolidation of team processes and cohesion. Then, as the team progresses in its development path, the coach would shift attention more towards the roles, their definitions and boundaries and conflict management mechanisms. Later, the emphasis would shift to the finer aspects of longevity, talent acquisition and management, goal refinement, output enhancement, etc.

The role of the team coach, unlike other forms of coaching in the organizational context, may be diagnostic and remedial. The possibility of the team leader being the team coach is as possible as the team coach being an outsider to the team.

As an outsider, the team coach's role is that of a catalyst in the team process than a reagent. Unlike the team leader, the outsider coach does not participate in the team processes but stays removed from it while facilitating its progress and growth in the right direction. He would be a real time non-participant observer and advisor, in some cases, as the director outside the scene of the activity. He would also be in a good position to provide the team with a credible and highly valid post facto analysis of the work, output and effectiveness of the team. The caution, however, is against him becoming and taking on the role of an external power centre to the detriment of the team.

The team leader as a coach himself has a hands-on feel of the goings on in the team. The closeness born out of being in the thick of the activity of the team with the members and participants in the activity would help the team leader have a real time sense of their thinking and mental makeup. He would be in a good position to work out the development and growth strategies for the team while being in the activity itself. While having this high advantage, there is also the need for the team leader to have the ability to distinguish between his role as the leader and that of a coach and be able to discharge both responsibilities without conflict or hinder to either roles. The leader as coach should also be in a position to command the respect of the members to take on the role of coach as well.

LIFE COACHING

The focus of life coaching tends to centre on the personal and social life of the individual. While Executive Coaching, workplace coaching and mentoring revolves around the professional aspects and features of the individual's life, life coaching takes on the aspects of the professional side of the individual's life to strengthen and build effectiveness in the personal and social space.

Table 2.1: Comparison of Individualized Development Interventions

Activity	Provider	Beneficiary	Objectives	Cost Mitigation
Counselling	Counsellor/ Psychotherapist	Individual	Regain functionality in life— often social and personal	Beneficiary
Mentoring	Senior/ Expert	Professionals	Transition in knowledge, thinking, work, life, etc.	Often gratis
Executive Coaching	Executive Coach	Senior executives/ Managers	Professional performance and effectiveness	Organization
Workplace Coaching	Coach/ Expert	Junior executives/ Non-executives	Skill development, knowledge enhancement, attitude engineering	Organization
On-the-job Coaching	Line Managers/ Supervisors	Workmen/ Non-executives	Skill development/ knowledge sharing	Organization/ part of job profile of provider

Life coaching targets enhancing the confidence and worth the individual feels about himself and his life. This approach aims at achieving emotional, cognitive and behavioural equilibrium and initiating changes when needed to attain personal goals and enhance the feeling of well-being and sense of worthiness about self. The key issues focused tends to work around work-life balance, building and maintaining functional and fulfilling relationships, equitable financial stability and ability to manage working towards a meaningful purpose in life and its fulfilment.

Life coaching practice works on assumptions regarding the coachee and his ability. There is the assumption that the coachee has the ability, resource and willingness to bring about changes that would ultimately help him lead a more fruitful and fulfilling life. The primary requirement being that there is an absence of mental health issues in the coachee and that the life coaching does not focus on therapeutic repair of psychopathologies that may exist.

Life coaching is solution-focused and works with the assumption that the coachee would be inclined to draw on his strengths and be willing to explore his hidden side in search for potentials as yet untapped. It also is preferred to be a structured process and with sufficient support systems built in to scaffold and assist the coachee in working out the changes planned. The structure and formality in the process is to the extent of it being functional with respect to the client. It does leave enough room for flexibility to head off any feeling of being constrained or pressured into conformity to the rigours of the process.

Life coaches may seek areas of specialization to work in, such as: working towards work-life balance; new directions in career and status; social and personal transitions and adjustments; clarifying sense of purpose in life; spiritual context in personal life; etc. The specializations often overlap and life coaches have a wide swath they claim as their area of specialty.

Life coaching ideally begins with the coach exploring the existing contours and dimensions of the life of the individual. Exploring the bottlenecks, barriers and constraints helps identify the problem areas. While working with the coachee to overcome these, the life coach also needs to get an adequate fix on the goals and picture the eventual destination in the process. The coach helps the individual actualize his aspiration through sustained search for clarity and determination to pursue his identified life goals.

The coach also works with the individual to figure out ways to keep on course in the medium and long term, during which period the coach may not be available.

Life coaching covers a wide sweep and the ability of the coach to cover the breadth of experiences and frames of references of their coachees is critical. Expertise in coaching apart, the depth and wisdom of the coach is the vital component in making life coaching successful.

The issue often encountered in life coaching revolves around being able to differentiate between the need for therapeutic psychotherapy and life coaching itself. Diagnostic and referral skills are frequently called to question in the choice of approach. Unlike life coaching, the therapeutic approach required in case of mental health issues in the client requires the intervention of qualified mental health professionals.

Life coaching requires no specific qualification or certification as an entry requirement. But a life coach should be able to recognize the need for the client requiring mental health aid when it comes up. Further, just as serious as the matter of qualification and certification is the issue of the quality of service offered by untrained or undertrained life coaches.

SKILL AND PERFORMANCE COACHING

Skill and performance coaching is perhaps the oldest and the original genre of coaching. This takes the form of helping young children acquire life and functional social skills, helping them enculturize to their surrounding community and comity of people. Almost in the same manner, skill and performance coaching approaches adult learning and development assisting the coachees acquire or develop and sharpen skills and capabilities. This leads in time to growing and enhancing competencies to elevate performance on the job.

This coaching is goal or target/task focused with the coachees determining the specifics at the skill level and working with the coach to define the parameters of success at the performance level. The role of the sponsors of the process also acquires importance in determining or calibrating the output and working out the possible timeframe.

Here the primary requirement is the capability and competence of the coach to deliver the targeted outcome in the process. The repertoire of the coach's abilities in helping the coachee imbibe, assimilate and be able to exercise the skill to enhance performance is central to the process. The coach should also have the aptitude to understand well the entry level of the coachee and design an appropriate process to meet the targeted outcome.

Aligning the requirements of skill development and performance enhancement with the internal desires and wishes of the coachee is another issue to be worked with at the start. Flowing from this is the design of the process. The learning design would depend on the learning style and preference of the coachee and also the preference of the coach.

Skill and performance coaching is one genre of coaching that can be subject to measurement and therefore calibrating the success in terms of the extent of skill acquisition and performance enhancement is the demonstrable element in it. These are assessable in a pre- and post-intervention longitudinal measurement.

The success of skill and performance coaching depends heavily on the ability of the coachee in applying himself to the task set out by the coach. The desire and motivation levels during the process are an important factor in the outcome. Therefore it devolves on the coach to monitor this in the coachee and work at keeping it high. The structure of the learning tasks, the understanding that the coachee has of it and the ongoing review and monitoring mechanism are just as important in influencing the success and outcome significantly. The coach's understanding of the learning styles and preferences help him choose an appropriate one for the coachee.

The time of engagement and the relationship between the coach and coachee may be limited to the set timeframe in the process. There is a chance of the relationship becoming that of a master and student with the authority structure building around it. While in some cases where it is mutually acceptable, this may be a functionally successful model, the tenor and character of relationship may tend to be more culture-dictated.

As long as there is sufficient clarity in the adoption of this form of engagement and genre of coaching, there is much to be gained by all connected. There cannot be additional burden of other expectations and desired outcomes loaded on this approach once it is underway.

DEVELOPMENTAL COACHING

Growth and development cannot be taken as mere attempt at change alone. It has to include some element of progress, improvement, expansion and movement towards the ideal in some form. Coaching towards acquisition of skills and enhancement of performance would satisfy the needs in the immediate or short-term. This has to be directed towards consolidation of the acquisitions into some patterns that persists in providing direction and further advancement, improvement and maturation.

Developmental coaching is a sort of natural progression from the skill and performance coaching. While skill and performance coaching aims to help the coachee imbibe specific skill sets and enhance demonstrable performance principally in the professional aspect of the coachee's life, developmental coaching works with a longer range of individual development. The focus is on the changes and growth that go beyond affecting only certain aspects of the coachee's life. A developmental coach looks to make the efforts cover the entire gamut of the coachee's life.

The range of issues worked with also is expansive and not restricted to any specific aspect. The focus shifts from mere problem solving capability to develop abilities to gain insights and conceptualize problem solving approaches to help deal with problems arising in future too.

The aim in developmental coaching tends to be set in the long term with the timeframe covering generally several years or even decades in the future. The changes and progress sought also tend to be more permanent in nature. This tends to make efforts and work in the developmental coaching take longer to fructify.

Table 2.2: Progression to Developmental Coaching

Skill Coaching	Performance Coaching	Developmental Coaching
Short term	Short to medium term	Longer term
Specific identified goals	Specific, but open goals	Evolving and growing goals
Addresses specific problem area	Addresses specific issue	Not restricted to issues or areas
Mastery over work	Aspirational	Holistic

Developmental coaching also seeks to arrive at a balance between the aspiration of personal development and the specific requests that may arise from the sponsors—the organization in most cases. The organization may expect through overt requests or being implicit in the sponsorship of the intervention of certain areas that need be addressed. The coach has to work out a balance between these and the needs of the coachee in adopting to work at developmental coaching. Certainly, choice of one over the other would not work well and the coaching intervention is itself at risk of breakdown.

Developmental coaching is worked at with the experience of the practitioners leading the way. There is no overarching theory in developmental coaching to guide the practice and therefore the wisdom, insights and the acumen of the coach tends to be the factors that affect the degree of success in practice. This also implies that the coach has the responsibility to keep the coachee and the sponsor—if there is any involved—briefed about the nature of the intervention and the centrality of the specific coach's role in it.

TRANSFORMATIONAL COACHING

Transformational coaching is working at the entire makeover of the individual coachee during the process. This is a transformation that may result in the coachee acquiring a completely new set of orientation, mooring and outlook in all aspects of his life. The process encompasses entire transformation and generally overhauling business, professional, career, social connectivity and life as such.

The agenda itself is set in a wide sphere and the timeframe may also accordingly be worked at in the long term. The ambitions in this effort are also high, the efforts required from both are immense and the risk also is commensurate with the stretched aspirations. In some sense, this is developmental coaching on high octane fuel.

The principal approach involves getting the coachee to become aware of, see, accept and work with a multitude of changes and makeover in personal, social and professional aspect of his life. From the coach, there is a high investment of energy, effort and determination in helping the coachee understand, believe in and internalize the transformation worked out. It also requires the coach to be able to concentrate and stay focused on the task taken up.

Underlying the approach is the crafting of the ability to get the coachee to invest adequately and accept ownership and buy-in for the process. The coach should have the ability to create a significant shift in the levels of learning of the coachee, thereby equipping him to acquire information and data and question assumptions and debate solutions. For someone working on a complete makeover, there has to be an appropriate convincing reason to embark on the effort and journey with someone helping in seeking the path.

There are other genres too—like Peer coaching, Career coaching, Leadership coaching, etc.—that would be of immense use in specific context. These do, however, get covered in some form in the ones discussed. Mentoring towers above all these in being one of the most powerful instruments for developmental intervention in the organization. It requires far greater preparedness and understanding and conducive conditions in the organization for it to take root and flourish. Mentors are, in a sense, higher level of beings than coaches and as such have to be taken as being in a different framework and employee development agenda.

Caselet 2 The Spiral of Confusion, Curiosity and Confidence

"How can I really feel comfortable sitting down across from someone I have no acquaintance with and pour out my life to him. How can I confide my feelings and intimate fear to him ..." Chirag Wadhwani had this running through his mind as he walked towards the Apollo Huddle Room in the fourth floor. "Now, it is easy for the 'bossman' and his HR cronies to think up of new ways to feel they are helping employees do better. I can understand training programmes and workshops, seminars and brainstorming sessions ... But this psychology mumbo-jumbo being thrown at us is the limit. If Arun, Meryl and the others have gone through this before, I should find out how they took it at all."

Chirag Wadhwani has grown in the Software Product Development Company rather quickly. He has been brilliant at his work and able to weave magic with the cutting edge product in mobile graphics application space. He has had phenomenal successes in the past few years with quite a few patents he could get filed. The rise in the company hierarchy also has kept pace with the growth of his brilliance and his increasing utility to the company.

The top team has singled him out for being given responsibilities in areas of product development that have high risk attached to it. His ability to inspire equally brilliant people in his work space would be critical in the design that the company has for him in the future. Raghav Ramanathan, the director and head of the Graphics Product Development team, has asked Chirag to come over for a meeting with the HR director to discuss the Executive Coaching plan being considered for him as an L&D initiative. The Executive Coaching is not new and the coach is also known to people in the company through quite a few years of successful association. Raghav had mailed a small brief to Chirag about Executive Coaching.

For people, it is important to know what they are getting into. A mail, a brief or even a formal notification without adequate background information and personal explanation often leads to key people not understanding what Executive Coaching is all about. They may even take it as being subject to some form of psychological intervention which sometimes carries a stigma that can well be done without. Much care and caution is best exercises before introducing people unaware of Executive Coaching to it. The most professionally proficient and socially savvy people are often not fully aware of the nature and characteristics of Executive Coaching.

----

3. EXECUTIVE COACHING: STRUCTURE AND PROCESS

IT WOULD NOT be wholly correct to say that coaching follows a sequential linear path. While there are discernable landmarks and milestones along the path, all too often one may have to double back to cover the tracks all over again—in some cases, several times. Not all processes follow the same path or the same set of markers. They all do need to go through broadly these stages to ensure a fruitful completion of the work and objectives set at the beginning.

The process discussed here is taking each stage in it separately and looking to describe it. However, in reality, these don't really come as integral or independent events. They tend to overlap or even double back to repeat some stages as the need and case may be. The process, in real life, tends to move like a coiled, self repeating spiral till the needs and objectives set out in the beginning are achieved. The discussion taking each as a separate event is to do with facilitating understanding.

THE START

A grand opening to the process is not essential but it is always good to mark a distinct starting point. Unlike the mentoring relationship, the coaching process is more purpose-driven with specifics in mind. The distinct starting point becomes all the more important when there is a need for an evaluation component to be put in place to measure the outcome and progress.

There may be an organizational requirement of tracking the number of contact sessions that have been conducted. In some cases, the contract with the coach is based on the number of contact sessions conducted. While this approach may not be the best of arrangements and would lay an unnecessary cumbersome burden on both the coach and the coachee, the organizational accounting process would find this pretty convenient.

Various terms are used to describe the beginning or the opening session—springboard, kick-off, inaugural, alpha session, etc. They all point to one purpose—the formal beginning of the coaching enterprise. This is true of all forms of coaching. Particularly in Executive Coaching, it is imperative to work at the commencement to prepare the executive to enter the process voluntarily.

Scheduling the springboard or kick-off session: the approach to this session varies depending on the organizational setting. The kick-off may be a forum to sell the idea of Executive Coaching as well to potential participants who, at times, do not have significant clarity about the intervention or the process.

In this case, it will be good to have some or all from the following list of people present and speaking at the kick-off session: senior management, former coachees, HR representative (process owner), L&D representative, the executive coach(es) and the prospective coachees. Some representation of the senior management team will go a long way in establishing the credibility of the intervention and also the seriousness of the investment being put into the intervention.

In addition, the kick-off session could have previous participants and beneficiaries from earlier interventions to share their experiences and views on the efficacy of the process. They could also contribute to, in a sense, preparing the new entrant and potential participants to the learning and change process they are embarking on.

The other party essential in the kick-off is the HR. They provide the stability and the foundation carrying the brief of making available any logistic support necessary. The HR being effectually the sponsor and the 'process owner', so to say, will have to make a statement of intent. The L&D representative, if they are not the direct 'process owner', should also be present as they provide the learning support that may go into the process at a later stage.

And then, there is the executive coach or coaches, as the case may be, along with the prospective coachees. The kick-off session is ideally an interactive one with the coach providing the brief for the process to come.

PREPARING FOR THE SPRINGBOARD OR KICK-OFF SESSION

For HR: Ensure that there is a senior management buy-in in the intervention. Brief the senior management stakeholders irrespective of whether they are attending the session or not. Specific brief to the stakeholders attending the meeting and launching the intervention at the springboard or kick-off session should be provided. The specific brief should include the background of the coach(es) involved and attending; the coaches included in the present intervention, preferably with an indication of the rationale for their inclusion; and list of other attendees invited indicating the involvement of these attendees with the Executive Coaching process. Including a write-up on the process with the experience of the organization with Executive Coaching will help the senior management stakeholder prepare for what he may want to say at the session.

From the HR side, it will also add tremendous value in giving a background to the attendees of the session regarding the approach taken by the organization in Executive Coaching and the support and assistance that can be expected from the HR during the intervention and after. The HR department must make it a point to be one of the people speaking at the kick-off session, if only to ensure ownership and responsibility for the intervention and establish its credibility in the process invested in.

Senior Management: A significant input into the success of the intervention is the way the top team stakeholders are seen to be valuing the intervention. It is not so much as the belief and the faith in the system as the demonstrated interest and investment put into it. It is important to showcase this as a priority high enough in the scheme of things for the top team in the organization.

It will be good to address the concerns that sometimes linger in the minds of those undergoing the coaching as to why the organization has chosen them for the intervention. The optimistic and confident among them take it as a great opportunity to enhance their repertoire of capabilities and competencies, but the concerns of those lower down on the confidence scale also need be addressed and their apprehensions dispelled. Some may see this as an attempt by the organization to point an accusing finger at their diminishing utility to the organization. These concerns, fears and misperceptions can be cleared by a statement from the senior management.

Speaking on the importance being placed on such an intervention not only builds the credibility of the effort, but also makes the unsure participants be convinced to invest greater effort and interest. The top team buy-in needs to be demonstrated by statements and, in later times, action by the top team itself, rather than being spoken of by someone else. The presence and the statements from the top-team stakeholders in the session gain considerable importance in this light.

It would also be good to touch upon the status of the coach(es) chosen for the intervention, his/their prior relationships with the organization and successes and any personal experiences with the coach in the past add much value.

Past Coachees: The primary role and the reason for suggesting the inclusion of former coachees is to provide a backdrop for the process, provide a testimonial and share their experiences with their peers. Having said that, their presence and role is often to extend help and support to alleviate small anxieties and concerns the new entrants may have. Sharing with openness their experiences enhances the credibility and builds realistic estimate of the expectations that can be built around the work being put in into the process. It will be good not to try to build positive bias by only talking about the obvious gains garnered in the process but to try and build a balanced picture of the effort required to be put in by the coachees, the sincerity, clarity of purpose and the caution that need to be exercised. Here, care must be taken not to overstretch the expectation. Emphasis must also be laid on the importance of the relationship and linkage with the coach.

Executive coach(es): The executive coach would have the brief from the HR and the profile of the prospective coachees already made available to him before the start of the process itself. The coach should ideally study the brief to catch any peculiarities that may need clarification at the start itself. The more meticulous he is in checking, the lesser the possibility of some hitch cropping up at a later stage.

He should prepare an overview of the Executive Coaching process itself. This is essential as the coachees would ideally like to hear the explanation of the process from the coach himself, even if they have been given any kind of handouts on the process by the HR. The coach should also highlight the expected gains form it, the work and the dedication that need to be put in, the duration that could be expected, the broad protocols of confidentiality and the relationship between the process and the organization and HR. The coach should be prepared to speak about himself, his background and his experience in the profession.

There is likely to be questions relating to the anxieties of the coachees before they enter the system. The coach should be in a position to quell any doubts and reassure them of the safety and the returns that can be expected. It would also be good to emphasize on the voluntary entry into the process and the need for the coachees to take responsibility for the drive and energy in the process.

PROTOCOL AND EXPECTATION-SETTING

The coaching relationship, like any relationship, has protocols that each in the relationship is to adhere to, to work towards the success of the relationship. Unlike other relationships, the context of the relationship is clear at the outset. Therefore the clarity of protocol is also essential at the start.

In this sense, both the coachee and the coach should be clear mutually and be aligned in their understanding of the relationship being entered into. The context is Executive Coaching and the relationship is that of the coach and the coachee. While this is clear, the finer aspects of the relationship need working on and articulated to head off any unnecessary burden being placed on it at a later date and circumstance.

For instance in the case of direct individual Executive Coaching, the terms of agreement regarding the duration, work to be done, the budgeting and cost, the approach and process should ideally be clarified and agreed upon at the outset. In the case of organization-sponsored Executive Coaching, the role of the executive coach in the context of the organization-setting, the position of the coachee in the coaching process, the role of the HR or the process owner, the organizational stand in coaching should be clarified and stated.

In both cases, the protocol with regard to confidentiality, the initial brief and the issue of responsibility should be articulated and mutual clarity arrived at before venturing into the process itself. The logistical details of how and where the contact sessions

Figure 3.1: Executive Coaching Process

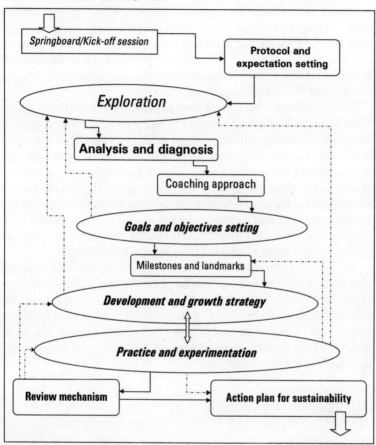

will be held, duration and procedure during the sessions and also the work to be done in the sessions should be stated clearly.

While the executive coach is the more experienced of the two in the coaching process and system, he would be the one to initiate and take the protocol setting forward. The broad contours of the protocol would be well-known to the coach, but it is necessary for both to work towards a common understanding and agreement at the start. The protocol-setting is not a legal or statutory session, but can be regarded as an essential part of the process.

Then again, it cannot be, nor is there the expectation, that the protocol would be in the nature of a contract, but the mutual understanding and agreement would serve to help each navigate and work through the intricate passages during the course of the coaching process. No document or paper need be created, but mutual acceptance is essential for the well-being and smooth conduct of the coaching process.

Now would also be a good time to state and clarify the expectations from the Executive Coaching from either side. Why is either of the parties entering into the process? What does either have in mind with regard to the outcome of the process and the role each will play in and during the process itself? For the coachee, it would serve to check out if his expectations are reasonable. This could be the expectation of the results to be expected, the role he is to play in the process, the help and assistance he can expect from the coach, how much work he would himself have to put in, the extent of openness he is expected, how to address his own comfort level, etc.

For his part, the executive coach could clarify his own expectation with respect to the work to be put in by the coachee; the role the coach himself will play in helping the coachee; the areas he would not be willing to work with or get into; the boundaries and limitations of the coaching process; the expectation of the position, status he expects, the seriousness expected to be invested by the coachee into the work; etc.

THE INITIAL SESSIONS

The initial sessions are often spent in getting to know the coachee. There are extensive explorations and discussions between the coach and the coachee covering the life of the coachee from the professional perspective. This includes the education and the time spent in the schooling, college, the early years in the profession, the growth and rise in the profession. It would do very well to also track any form of professional courses, degrees and any form of training that the coachee may have taken up during the professional career.

The coach would then like to look at the direction that the coachee would have taken in the initial years and look at the rationale for this and the direction in the later years, the thinking and the calculation that would have led to these choices.

Essentially, the coach is trying to get in touch with the kind of thinking that has led the coachee up to the point of getting into coaching.

Whatever the form and objectives of the Executive Coaching effort, the clearer the picture the coach and the coachee are able to get about the lead up to this point in time, the better the plan and strategy for the future can be. It is for this reason that the executive coach spends a significant time in the initial sessions to explore the life of the coachee along with him.

The executive coach may also want to generate some form of data from certain questionnaires and psychometric tests that he feels the coachee could take. These tests and data generated from them serve to get a clearer and more accurate perspective on the coachee and the issues that exist at the start of the process. The kind of tests and nature of the instrument would be best left to the executive coach to figure out in his best judgement.

The exploration inevitably leads on some form of diagnosis of the state of the professional stage the coachee is in now and a broad picture of the changes that may be needed in the process of development that can be planned. This is often the initial picture to set the coachee thinking on what can be expected and the choices that may be available to him during the process. The idea of diagnosis would indicate some form of malady or distortion that exists. However, this not being the case, the diagnosis is intended to be a study of the present state of the coachee and any corrective action or change that may immediately be needed or can be visualized upfront. This diagnosis is what may lead to further plans of action as the process goes forward.

As the process progresses through more detailed and granular exploration, the subtleties of the image of the possible future emerge. At some point in time, the executive coach may find himself adequately equipped to take on the next stage of the process ahead of exploration and diagnosis.

DECISION ON APPROACH

It is at this stage that broadly the decision of what approach should be taken in the coaching process has to be worked upon. The decision need not be unilateral and exclusively depending on the judgement of the executive coach. He may also choose to work with the inputs that the coachee, or for that matter somebody else, may provide. His concern is in working out what would be in the best interest of the coachee, the progress in the process and the optimal outcome from the intervention.

The major factors intervening in this decision would be the profile of the coachee, his preferred learning style, the time available for the intervention and the ambience and environment within which the Executive Coaching is taking place. Also the preference and expertise of the coach would come into play in choosing the approach.

The approach is not a binding decision that has to be carried along till the end of the intervention. It can be dynamically changed depending on the changing needs of the coachee and the judgement of the coach. There may be instances of multiple approaches being woven together to suit the needs of the process. Different approaches may be employed to meet the needs arising out of the different contexts within the coaching process.

CALIBRATING GOALS

Some coachees come into the intervention with definite goals and targets set to be achieved in the time and effort invested. Some have a direction in mind and will need help in working out the clear goals and destination. There may also be others who have no definite goal in mind but do intend to use the opportunity and investment to get better than they are now. Whichever the case, the need is to progress and work towards improving their capabilities and enhancing their effectiveness in all or any aspect of their life. Having come in voluntarily, they would be willing to invest some interest and energy into the process.

Goals are ideally thought out by the coachee with the help of the executive coach rather than worked out by the coach, and either co-opted or accepted by the coachee. Most executive coaches work with the senior members in the organization who would be independent-thinking people and well-established by themselves. They are capable of working through the process or seeking the right goals and target themselves, with a little help from the executive coach playing a facilitative role.

Few would expect goals to be spelt out for them. Most would prefer the coach evaluating the goals and offering suggestive comments on the goals. The role of the executive coach in this depends on how the coach sees his role in the process. There are preferred styles among executive coaches on how the goals are worked out.

Then again, the goals worked out or fixed at this stage may not be specific, clear or even tangible. They may be just directions for movement or work, or, in some cases, identification of work to be done in the context of development in the coachee. It may be decided to keep the goals fluid and flexible and, in some cases, dynamic as the process progresses. There could also be instances of preferring to not work with specific goals and leave the process open with the intent of developing in any direction that works well in the perspective of the executive coach and the coachee.

The need for the goal is as much in the nature of having a target to shoot for as it is a means of calibrating progress as the process gets underway. The choice not to have goals in the Executive Coaching process is also a done thing. The process is not adrift but is deliberately left open to seek and work at any opportunity and direction that may be the best available. The coachee is willing to leave the specifics to evolve as the process progresses. While keeping options open, the coach and the coachee are also bearing in mind that the energy required to work without goals and targets are enormous and may turn out to be taxing. The need is to be able to differentiate between working with several options at the same time and being adrift. Here, both the executive coach and the coachee should be in agreement with the choice being made and also the mechanics involved in moving forward with having taken such a course.

The goals set may also entail revisiting the choice of approach to be followed during the rest of the process. The approach in Executive Coaching that has worked well in determining and getting a fix on the goals may not necessarily be the ideal for the working towards and achievement of the goals. This would require careful consideration and the wisdom of the executive coach in figuring out which approach is likely to suit the process with all the intervening factors mentioned earlier and also work in achieving the goals with the coachee.

IDENTIFYING MILESTONES

Having goals and targets is one thing, but being sure that the path travelled and the speed being right is quite another thing. It is for this purpose that landmarks and milestones to be logged are worked out during the process.

Each goal and objective will be worked towards at a pace of its own. The work being done may be parallel or linear depending on what the executive coach feels the coachee should embark upon. Therefore, it would be good to have each goal and target handled independently first and the pace measured for itself.

There is also the need to keep the overall picture in view and see how the progress in one relates to the other. Whether they are complimenting each other, working in coordination or sapping too much energy working at the same thing multiple times, is something that needs to be monitored. For this, the clearer the landmarks and milestones are figured out, the easier the task of keeping tabs on progress will be.

WORKING OUT STRATEGIES

This is the job that is at the heart of testing the capabilities of the executive coach. It is this that would differentiate an excellent executive coach from the others in the trade. It is the astute ability to figure out what would work well for the coachee keeping in view his profile, capability, drive and desire and the goals being targeted.

The executive coach spends much of the time working with the coachee to customize the work strategies to fit well the needs of the coachee and ensure the drive towards success holds to the end. Under normal circumstances, the coach spends time analyzing the information he has garnered about the coachee in the preceding sessions, the briefs he has been given and the coachee's own declaration. This works to give him the picture of how the coachee would operate under conditions that will arise in the working of the strategies that will be needed.

Most executive coaches work with the instinct honed over years of practice and may not have set patterns or a well-worn path to be followed. Ask any coach and he will not be able to predict how the strategy will typically come through. Often, it is a combination of theoretical possibilities and instinctual reading of the coachee that works here. There is really no best strategy for any particular goal set. However, the executive coach will be able to tell in no uncertain terms what would work well and what would not come through.

This is more likely to be true in the case of life coaching. In skill and performance targets, there could be some beaten tracks and set paths that can be followed. There could also arise some form of commonalities or careers running along similar tracks among coachees, but the individual differences make cloning of strategies a really bad idea. In developmental and transformational coaching areas, the difficulty is compounded by the complexities of issues arising out of idiosyncrasies of each coachee. This tests the capabilities and the judgement of the executive coach to the limit at times.

Getting a fix on the strategies up ahead helps getting a perspective on what is possible and also relooking at the feasibility of the goals being sought to be reached. This would also be a good time to revisit the choice of the approach and the recalibration of goals if necessary. It would also give a good measure of the effort and the energy that would be needed from both the coach and the coachee in getting to where both have decided they want to go.

Then again, the strategies for the work to be done in the process at this stage are not set in stone, and so can be amended or updated as the need may be along the way. The plans at this stage are the ones that give a good lift-off for the effort being invested. They would need to be evaluated and monitored as the process gets underway.

One of the key things that need to be remembered in the strategy formulation is the provision for scaffolding the efforts of the coachee in the change and development process so as the help prop up the new while it takes shape and hardens to stand on its own. These may come in the shape of taking the support and help of significant others, resolutions to persist or, in some cases, a mechanism of reward and punishment being put in place.

PRACTICE AND EXPERIMENTATION

Between the coach and the coachee, the strategies are worked out to reach the set goals at the earliest and in the easiest manner. This requires the coachee working out along the decided path. The attempt is to ensure that any change planned is tried out,

tested and then internalized. In different approaches, the requirements from the coachee differ to some degree. This indicates that
the coachee will have to practice the planned behavioural, learning or attitudinal change being tried out over a set period of time
to check its applicability and efficacy before deciding to carry it
along, or to abandon it for something else.

The possibility is also that there would be a need for experimenting with different changes and deciding on which one suits
best. The stage of practice and experimentation by the coachee
will also generate enough understanding and data to see how
the strategies are working out and if there needs to be any form
of change or shift in the strategy itself. Any development effort
requires trying out the new and then figuring out the means to
internalize and sustain the best result.

The coach and the coachee try, over a set period of time, the
different strategies of change and progress they have charted for
the coachee. The experimental behaviour, attitude, outlook, skill
or even perception could be a turn for the better for the coachee
and therefore worth persisting with. Such successes are retained
while the rest weeded out in the practice and experimentation at
this stage.

REVIEW MECHANISM

The review mechanism is set to take stock of the progress along
the decided lines, meeting the set landmarks and milestones, the
extent of learning or change in the coachee and efficacy of the process itself. The review mechanism is to be built into the process
also as a feedback to both the coachee and the executive coach.

The review mechanism can also be in the form of any evaluation that may be built into some of the process by choice. The
evaluation helps to audit the efficacy of the intervention itself. The
evaluation part is ideally done at the completion of the intervention. However, the preferred mode is to set the review as a con-
tinuous element in the process so as to keep constant tab on the
progress in the process.

The review is also ideally to be done bilaterally rather than being undertaken by the executive coach or the coachee alone, or
even the process owner by himself. The credibility of the review
data will be higher if the review is an open process. The review

may also throw up possible issue of needing to explore deeper into understanding the coachee better. The review is also intended as a sort of a quality check in the Executive Coaching system.

ACTION PLAN FOR SUSTAINABILITY

Any intervention should be planned and executed in such a manner that the benefits of it endure. The Executive Coaching is one such high value intervention. There is so much of effort, time and resources invested in it and there is so much of expectation from it not only from those involved but also the other related stakeholders that there is a strong need for working out means of making the outputs last longer.

It is for this reason that the intervention should ideally plan and execute ways of ensuring sustainability of the gains from it. This effactully forms the last step in the process. The sustainability plans are in the nature of some unwritten agreement or contract between the executive coach and the coachee on how the follow-up and follow-through of the work put in will be carried forward. These take the form of periodic revisitations, refresher meetings, exercises and activities that refresh the learning, the long-term steps that need to be executed over a period of time, etc. Under normal circumstances, the action plans are worked out with some time frame also built into it so that there could be continued monitoring and review as well.

The different stages in the Executive Coaching process merge into the next seamlessly and the flow is normally smooth when the executive coach is experienced enough to understand and carry it through. There may sometimes be a few hiccups or difficulties when the issues involved are contentious. But then the means of handling them are usually built into the way the process proceeds.

The process also has certain inbuilt mechanisms to ensure that the efficacy of the output is taken care of. This is often by doubling back in the loop within the process and reviewing each result as they are worked out.

4. PREPARING TO BE COACHED

PREPARING TO ENTER the realm of coaching as a coachee has more to do with engineering attitude and approach than either with logistics or tasks to be done. Entering the intervention with the right frame of mind can lead to far greater takeaways than otherwise. A walkthrough of the preparatory steps can configure the mind positively towards working smoothly and maximizing the returns in Executive Coaching.

Executive Coaching is not an L&D intervention that can be walked into blindly. It does require some preparation. And then, the prior preparation is not something to be done similar to entering into a training programme. It requires much more attitudinal orientation than information updation.

A good place to start would be to look up available literature and write-ups on coaching as a learning process in organizations. While the number of books abound, it will be prudent not to devour so much at the start so as to begin with an intellectual indigestion. Go easy on the reading; catch up on short articles before settling on to self-help books. The more academic and scientific ones are best saved for when you have the coach available to discuss the technical and complex aspects of Executive Coaching.

Being informed about Executive Coaching best serves to understand what one is walking into, the contours of the process, the roles the coach and coachee play, the relationship between them and, most important, how to maximize the return on the investment being made in the effort.

It is important that the coachee understands well the Executive Coaching process because the better and clearer the sequence and logic, the easier the effort being put in will be to the coachee. Consequently, the results and takeaways from it could be optimized. Further, while the executive coach would chart a course in the best interest of the coachee, initiative and informed voluntary effort from the coachee adds value and facilitates the process moving smoothly forward and at an optimum pace.

IS EXECUTIVE COACHING THE NEEDED INTERVENTION?

Having understood the process and the requirements, it would also augur well to see if such a development process is the needed and appropriate one at this point in time. While Executive Coaching could be beneficial for the individual, it is not necessarily the best learning and development intervention in all cases.

If the L&D approach is intended to address a specific issue or problem with respect to the individual, the L&D solution should be appropriate for it. There are several factors contributing to the success of Executive Coaching, for example: Executive Coaching requires adequate time and the right orientation in the coaches and coachees; the environment and atmosphere in the organization should be conducive to foster the effort; the post-intervention environment should support the implementation of the intended result and accommodate the consequent changes adopted; among other factors. A mismatch in any of these could lead to the result ranging from inadequate to disastrous. Misreading the need for Executive Coaching before entering into it is ill advised. Then again, Executive Coaching should not be taken as a universal solution for all learning and development ills in the organization. Earlier chapters discuss the conditions and circumstances where Executive Coaching can be best used and where it is best avoided.

KNOW THE EXECUTIVE COACH

Getting to know the executive coach helps much with the preparedness. It gets a measure of the kind of person one will be dealing and working intimately with.

The executive coach would, for his part, be seeking an initial brief and a profile of the coachee at the start of the intervention. Along the same lines, it would be prudent to seek initial introductory information about the coach as well. However, the caution to be exercised is that in seeking information about the coach, guarding against planted negative or positive bias would be a good idea. This is best achieved through checking and ascertaining the credibility of the source of the information and the source's own motive in supplying the information.

Within the organizational context, the HR would have walked through the process of checking out the executive coach in terms of references, prior work, etc. In this case, the HR would be a good point to begin with in getting information about the executive coach. Otherwise, it will be well advised to do a search, check websites, brochures, provided literature, etc.

In cases where there is no prior exposure to the executive coach, either through peers, friends or other organizational contacts, it will be good to begin with reviewing the professional credentials of the coach. Seeking information on the professional background and work will be a good idea. If references are provided, a chat with the referee could provide valuable insights into what to expect in working with the coach.

Getting to know something about the coach will be comforting in understanding the extent of compatibility possible with the coach. Knowing the past experience of the coach can help dispel and mitigate any possible risk that you may be walking into.

Another good step to take would be to validate the claims of confidentiality assured by both the process and the specific coach. This is more on the lines of seeking your own assurance and then checking the ethical compliance by the coach in earlier cases, though both are as important.

In the process of checking out the coach, unanswered questions may come up. Taking note of them, not only to track but also to seek answers to them at a later date when the contact with the executive coach would be closer, would be a good idea.

CHECKING OWN PREPAREDNESS

Getting into Executive Coaching is not as easy a process as entering a walk-in intervention in L&D. For any degree of success and to derive any form of positive output from the intervention, preparedness is essential at the very beginning. This is not something that can evolve as the process gets underway. Not meeting the basics of preparedness puts a heavy burden of unnecessary stress of extra work on the coach. It may also lead to unpredictable and undesired turns midway through the intervention. Rather, check preparedness at the very outset than risk failure or less than desired output from a high-investment effort.

Here is a checklist of preparedness before entering Executive Coaching as a coachee. Are you:

- interested in personal development
- willing to put in effort without direct supervision
- willing to work on commitments
- willing to introspect
- willing to be open to criticism
- willing to share
- willing to establish close rapport without reciprocal sharing
- willing to work at building trust
- willing to acknowledge own failures/weakness/unresolved issues
- willing to experiment
- willing to change
- willing to put in extra effort where called for
- willing to explore personal space
- willing to relook at relationships
- willing to question, affirm or reject long-held beliefs
- have spoken with others who have already undergone Executive Coaching

CHECK TIME SCHEDULE OVER THE INTERVENTION PERIOD

Coaching is about commitment to the process and giving it the priority so as to make it effective. Knowing that the intervention will last over a certain period of time, the best thing to do would be to ensure that during that period, your other commitments could be reset to accommodate the time needed to take on the coaching.

Caselet 3 Missing the First Bus

March has never been the best of months. February too leans more towards March with just as unfavourable a disposition. Ravindran Nair always felt the stress of the season to be pretty unbearable every year. But then this year the torrent of work, deadlines and sales targets threatens to wash everything and everyone downstream!

"However much one may prepare early for the rush of work, it does not prevent fate from changing the rules", rues Ravindran. "I had worked out my schedule well and had prepared to fit in my work with the executive coach along with the regular rush that was expected. But then, I did not expect that the organization would decide to restructure my division, bifurcating it to manage better the portfolio my division was handling.

"And being the head of the division, this activity took up my entire time to work out the team and product division between the class and mass differentiation. I was working 16 hours each day for weeks on end. I had to cut a sorry figure with the coach. I could not face him to tell him that I had to drop out of the programme. He had so much hope in my ability to do well and we had great plans for my learning and future in career. I told the HR head that I will not be able to face the coach after letting him down so badly. This was one thing I could not forgive myself for, but then, what choice did I have?"

The Head of HR of the Business Unit was disappointed and also upset at the stand taken by Ravindran.

"He is senior enough to realize what sort of example he is setting for members of his team. We had gone through so much trouble to get the executive coach to work for us and had fixed the schedule with so much care. Nair should have had the courtesy to atleast take the responsibility to meet with the executive coach to let him know, or at the very least, apologise for the constant absence from sessions and upsetting everyone. All the other in the group have gone ahead and we can see so much they have gained from working around tight schedules and targets. I felt let down so much by Nair."

That was six months ago. Ravindran could see other colleagues and peers doing well for having put in the investment in Executive Coaching intervention that the organization had sponsored. In September, Ravindran asked to meet with the executive coach once again on his own time to see if they could restart the process. For the following nine weeks, Ravindran had made it a point to keep all appointments scheduled with the executive coach; even going to the extent of flying across the country to spend the committed time of a few hours with the coach when the call of work had kept him away from the city.

"Ravindran with his born-again faith in Executive Coaching had gained more by far than others in the group, all because he had made it a point to invest in the effort needed the second time around. Realizing what has been missed sometimes work well in making people work harder to make up," says the executive coach.

Often, the bane of the process is to vacillate, postpone or call off committed coaching dates and timings. It not only affects the rhythm and the planned schedule, but also works to the detriment of the final outcome of the intervention itself. Further, unless the executive coach is patient and is willing to work with the disturbed routine, the investment from his side will be affected as well.

Check to see if there are any major projects or personal commitments during the period that could compete in some way for attention, mindspace and time with the Executive Coaching commitments. If these are not ones that can be rescheduled and are of primary importance, then it would be good to take a call to rework the period and schedule for entering the Executive Coaching intervention itself.

Most often, the schedule, with dates and timings for the contact sessions along with the approximate time that needs to be committed for the intervening work that comes with the intervention, could be worked with the executive coach well in advance. Finding out the commitments needed and then working out the schedule with the executive coach in advance would save embarrassments and ill will later on.

CONSOLIDATE PERSONAL INFORMATION

Almost every Executive Coaching intervention begins with the sharing of personal information with the coach so as to get him familiar with the subject he is working with. The initial few sessions are about the sharing and exploration of the individual and his professional, personal and, often, social space.

Being unprepared, these initial sessions tend to meander through issues and pieces of information forgotten or mislaid. The clearer the picture that the coach can derive of the individual in these initial sessions, the easier, smoother and, often, more productive the later sessions would be. A good way to approach this would be to work a pathway to navigate these initial sessions.

Begin with the professional life. Walk the executive coach through the early years of your career, stay with information first, giving data and pointing to significant happenings. The different organizations or major departments you have moved through and experienced. The kind of professional track record you have logged up. Staying with the narration of facts initially helps the executive coach in not having to sift through perspectives and opinions unless he needs them to understand anything of significance he has noticed.

Give your analysis of the route you have taken in your professional life after you have acquainted the executive coach with the facts and happenings. Leave it to the coach to interpret and conclude things out of what you have given him.

It will be good to follow this up with the details of early life and the kind of family and environment you come from. Details of your parents and siblings help the executive coach understand your background better. Here, it would be also good to share any significant events or happening you have experienced in the early part of life that you feel has contributed in shaping you. The immediate family, spouse, children and the environment at home is also a significant thing to share.

The issues in personal life does not necessarily become relevant in the Executive Coaching intervention unless it has any direct bearing to the kind of professional choices you have made. However, it will be good to share as much as you are comfortable with with the executive coach so as to give him a holistic picture of the person you are.

To complete the picture, it will be a good idea to include the social aspects of your life and the circle of friends you keep and the nature of your social interaction and life. The extent of details you may want to share is a discretionary call you can take depending on how you are disposed to the idea of sharing them with your coach.

Being prepared with the details and even going to the extent of drawing up a list of information, perspectives and ideas you would like to share will cut down the time, effort and the unnecessary dialogue that is likely to take place in the initial sessions of the Executive Coaching process. Spend some time initially, before the session, to consolidate this information, working out in your mind the details you intend to share, those you intend not to share and also those you intend to ask the executive coach about before deciding whether you want to share or not.

Caselet 4 **Through the Cloud of Fog**

Dr Hans Batra had sat in the back row towards the far end of the conference room at the kick-off session, almost as if he was standing out and looking in at the meeting. He had maintained a silence throughout the session. He appeared to listen intently to all that was being said and discussed. He was observing the executive coach keenly. There was something that was on his mind and it was bothering him. Decision on this one did not come easily to him.

All the same, he thought he might as well give it a try. After the meeting, when everyone had left, he walked up to the executive coach. He told the coach that he would like to spend some time with him before he can take a call on whether he wanted to join the group who had opted to begin the Executive Coaching association from the following week.

"I have given this thing a lot of thought before coming in today," Dr Batra began. "I'm not sure anyone has any solution to my list of problems and troubles. But I want to ask you a few questions before I can decide on anything. Can I ask them?" The executive coach said the obvious, "Sure. Let's find some place to sit quietly."

Dr Hans Batra thoughtfully followed the executive coach back into the conference room to a quiet corner. Once seated, Dr Batra began, "I think I am doing fairly well as far as my work is concerned… Maybe, I can make a few changes, but that is not at all my concern. I have to ask you some questions about what can be done in the coaching exercise."

The executive coach encouraged Dr Batra to continue. "Go on…" he urged.

"Let me list the questions I have in my mind so that I can decide whether I want to take up the coaching at all as a prescription for my problems", Dr Batra continued. "First, I want to know how confidential will the information and discussion be. You had said that the discussions will be only between you and me. But I want to be sure. Maybe I'm being too cautious. But even then…"

He paused, but did not wait for the executive coach to reply. He continued on: "My problems are personal and they are troubling me in my work. I have issues at my home, with my family, with their health and such matters. So my second question is, does the coaching have to be related to work alone? Can I search for solutions for my other problems too? And then, I myself have issues with my health.

"I have difficulty understanding why I am here even now. I have a great job and am doing great, but I should never have returned to India after my post-doc. I had so many great offers too. But the health of my wife, my family … And now my health too. And to add to this, my brother and properties. See, I'm pretty muddled about my issues and troubles as well. So, my third question—if I myself am confused about what I want, how will someone else help me?"

All the words tumbled out in one quick gush. Dr Hans Batra seemed almost relieved at the end of it.

"Oh, you have already gone through quite a bit of what would have been the first session," the executive coach told Batra.

"If affirmative assurance of help is all that's holding you back, you should walk right in… All these answers you are looking for can be sought right there in the process if you are willing to work your way through it. I'll walk with you all the way. Think about it, Dr Batra."

TRACK OBJECTIVES IN ENTERING EXECUTIVE COACHING

Before entering into the Executive Coaching scheme, it would be good to have a set of objectives of your own. While it is normal for objective-setting to be done in consultation with the executive coach, starting with what you have in mind always helps sharpen the objectives being mutually set. Most coaches do ask the coachee if there is anything they may have in mind before working on setting out objectives to be pursued in the process.

There are also some important things to be borne in mind while approaching this. Setting objectives do help but be open to changing or recalibrating them during the process itself. Then again, the goals and objectives set before the commencement of the process may not be comprehensive. Therefore, it is important to accept this fact and be willing to take on added objectives and goals as the process moves forward.

In setting objectives for yourself, review the needs you have been experiencing over the recent past in the work you have been involved in. Track any inadequacies and feeling of not being up to the tasks you find yourself faced with. And then focus on what other competencies or skills that will help you achieve higher and better results not only at work, but also in other aspects of your life.

Having the objectives in mind also helps the coachee track the progress of the coaching intervention as it moves forward. This proactive move is beneficial for not only the coachee but also helps the executive coach understand better the needs and the motivation of the coachee in the intervention.

TRACK POTENTIAL ISSUES AND CONCERNS

As with the objectives, so it would be with significant issues and concerns that are at the forefront of the coachee's consciousness. Most of the people have unresolved issues that are banked for addressing at a later date. These could be for reasons of not having the adequate time, not being important enough at this time, not knowing how to deal with or resolve them now or just plain not having cared enough about them. These issues tend to clog the expressway of our consciousness, clutter mindspace and often leading to unseen stress and slowing down.

Such issues sometimes have not even been identified by the individual at this point in time. It is good to have these issues and concern addressed and taken care of either by resolving them or by learning to manage them better.

The executive coach would be better at identifying potential issues or existing sores that fester. He also would be better equipped to walk the coachee towards resolution or suggest action to mitigate the negative impact of these issues—either working through them or parking them in non-interfering ways. Though the executive coach is better equipped, identifying potential issues and concerns ahead of meeting him always helps and makes the process easier to work with.

TRACK BUDGET AND RESOURCE INVESTMENT

Tracking budget would be necessary when the contract in the Executive Coaching is between the individual and the coach. This will be normally taken care of by the HR in the organizational context. However, it would be a good practice to keep in mind what is being invested in the effort. Here, the investment is not only in terms of the professional fees being paid to the coach, but also the extent of investment that has gone into the whole intervention, in terms of the monetized value of the time, effort and the missed opportunities.

When the individual has a direct contract with the coach, the best is to be clear about the cost and terms of the transaction at the outset rather than it becoming an issue in the midst of the process itself. Then again, there may be other resources that may be needed in terms of the logistics, travel and other expenses that may need to be accounted for. Getting an understanding on these is out of the way before the intervention starts off in right earnest is ideal.

KEEP FAMILY AND SIGNIFICANT OTHER IN THE LOOP

There are strict ethical issues in the Executive Coaching intervention. Confidentiality is one of the major factors that not only contribute to the success of the process, but also ensure that parties involved are comfortable in working together.

The executive coach may have preferences of his own, but normally in the coaching process, the coachee is encouraged to keep the significant people in their life in the loop about being in and going through the process, particularly, the members of the family, immediate colleagues and any significant others in the social circle.

Caselet 5 Who Waved the Wand?

Srilakshmi came straight to the point. "I have been married to Venkat for the past 14 years. I have known him for nearly seven years before that. We had been college mates and then colleagues in our previous company. So I can say I know Venkat through and through."

I was meeting her in the conference room at the Corporate Office along with her husband Narayanan Venkateswaran, Senior Vice President in charge of Research and Development (R&D). Srilakshmi had requested to come along and meet me during our usual early morning sessions that was mutually convenient. Venkateswaran had signed up to be a part of the group comprising senior management of the R&D set-up of the organization. While others in the group had been slow and worked steadily at evolving their coaching strategies, Venkateswaran was sort of a man possessed. He had insisted on sessions scheduled more often. He was unrelenting in experimenting with new and different styles and even went to the extent of trying out changes in his dress and physical appearance.

Venkateswaran was not maladjusted by any stretch of imagination. He had led a professionally successful but otherwise ordinary life. The only time he appeared to have stepped out of line was in the choice of Srilakshmi as wife. For this, he had stood up against his entire family, and even for a time had been ostracized for the act. His keen intellect and sharp mind were his assets and he had used them to work well and rise up in the hierarchy in the organization and command respect in the fraternity. To all around, he was as predictable a person as there can be. Even his wife had taken this as the permanent script.

"When I had told Srilakshmi that I was getting myself an executive coach to help me with a makeover, she had smiled. I could almost hear her say, 'Ah…right! …You? And makeover?... Let's see...' Well, that's what gave me the idea of seeing if there was any limit to how much I can re-make myself to being better and do most of the things I had given up on as 'not possible' for me."

Venkateswaran had confided. "I had always shared all that we discussed in the contact sessions with Srilakshmi, always, as you had suggested. Initially she was sceptical, then tolerant, and as she began to see changes I could bring about, she finally became a believer."

Srilakshmi says, "For somebody who had changed little as a person in 20 years, he has suddenly transformed himself. Today he not only comes along for our morning walks, he is also talking most of the time. Earlier I was the one who did 90 per cent of the talking at home. Venkat even has suggestions on what we can cook... Do you believe it? For someone who never used to even notice what he ate, he has become a food critic now... I am getting calls from his colleagues congratulating me on transforming Venkat at work too. They all somehow think I am responsible… But I wanted to see who has really helped in this remarkable transformation. That's why I wanted to meet you."

This has to do with the fact that during the process of Executive Coaching, it is very likely that the coachee would undergo changes in behaviour, outlook and attitude. It is most likely to affect those in the close immediate circle around the coachee. It is better that they be informed that the changes are a part of a planned, deliberate attempt rather than a random occurrence. This protects the coachee against any possible adverse fallout of the changes adopted and also helping him adapt himself to the reactions of the people around him.

Further, it would also work well in enlisting the assistance of the people around him if need be. This comes in particularly handy where there is a need to elicit feedback from the people around on either the individual or the impact of changes being attempted during the process.

PREPARE TO LOG LEARNINGS

Executive Coaching is a longitudinal process that is spread over time. The insights and learning garnered too are not a one-step event. They come in bits and pieces and, sometimes, in innocuous packages. All too often, they tend to be missed in the bustle of other happenings not only in the Executive Coaching process but also in the active life at work.

These insights into oneself, perspectives on plans and strategies for the future, new learning and ideas, recognition of growth and development in thinking, clarity and speed in thought process and ideation, etc., come in unannounced and at unexpected times. Holding on to these are a vital part of the Executive Coaching process. Hence, learning to log these as they come by to capture and register them becomes an essential skill to be imbibed early in the process.

The executive coach would, in all probability, encourage the coachee to take up the task of keeping tabs on the learning and ideas generated during the discussions and at other times. Keeping log also helps in tracking events during the process, especially where any form of experimentation in behaviour or attitude change is being worked upon. The preparedness of the coachee in being systematic and regular in keeping and maintaining log of the learning enhances the positive takeaway from the intervention.

Caselet 6 A Beacon in the Darkness

Dear Sir,

I remember we had many friendly arguments about your insistence on my not calling you 'Sir'. And you will recall that I had argued that in Indian culture, you are my Guru and I will reserve the right to call you 'Sir'. That is why I am still staying with calling you 'Sir'. Hope you will find it within yourself to forgive me for this some day.

I am writing to share with you the good news of my taking over as Executive Director yesterday at Innovation Drug Delivery Research Limited. The discussion I have been having with the company over the past few weeks has finally come through. I had spoken with you about this in our conversation couple of weeks ago.

What is significant for me to share with you is that during the unpleasant months I had in the previous company, your advices and directions were a source of inspiration and confidence for me. While I spent a lot of time with my Spiritual Guru and he has given me the strength to bear the last few months in that organization, our discussions had really helped me stay on course and work tirelessly towards my goal.

I still remember your words, "Think CEO, don't peg your aspirations any lower". Lots of times I was tempted to give in and take easy offers, but your coaching has helped me stay on through difficult times. In particular, I must say what I had thought to be a really childish instruction to an adult had been my biggest gain because I followed the instruction.

As you remember, I had followed the instruction and had made it a point to write down everything we discussed, all the observations and activities in between sessions, and also made notes of our contact sessions. The learning and the motivation you had spoken off in the sessions were what I used to read regularly when I found myself feeling down. I am so happy that I have learnt and have made it a habit to take notes during and after each session. That has been my biggest gain.

Even going through the notes when I am free helps refresh the discussion in my mind and that is the best legacy from the Executive Coaching sessions. I am sure I will also try to get my team to begin the habit early in their careers.

I am writing to thank you for all your support, good wishes and helping me gain the strength to work through troubled times. In one way, I owe this position I am taking over to my spiritual Guru and to you.

Thank you once again, Sir,
Respectfully yours,
Dr Kartik Pandian

MOVING FORWARD

There is a specific and identifiable end to the contact part of the process in Executive Coaching. There will come a time in the process when the Executive Coach and the coachee will have to plan a process of delinking and working towards moving ahead. The coachee will have had the confidence to walk forth on his own and look at managing the process largely on his own.

Shedding the dependence of the coachee on the advice, perspectives and thinking of the executive coach is a part of the process. This has to be mutually worked out and agreed upon in ideal times. The coachee must also look forward to working this out when he feels the confidence to manage the process of his own development and learning himself.

There may also be a time when the need is to move beyond the present executive coach to working with someone more specialized in the tasks and plans that come in the future. Working this transition to be as seamless as possible helps all the parties involved in the process. The preparation required of the coachee is to be aware of the need and look at how best it can be worked out. How the sustenance of the relation with the executive coach can be carried forward fruitfully into the future is to be kept in mind. The coachee can, through mutual consent, also work out a schedule of meeting into the future as well if the terms earlier agreed upon fit into this scheme.

Understanding the process, at least in terms of what to expect from it, the work involved and preparing for it makes for taking the steps forward to get the best out of being a part of the intervention. Rather than enter blind, it is good to walk in prepared. All too often, the initial preparation is what gets the best out of the coachee as well. It eases the executive coach's work in the process and thus helps him focus on better inputs and learning for the coachee. In L&D interventions, efforts invested early always brings in far better dividends.

5. COMPETENCIES, CAPABILITIES AND SKILLS FOR EXECUTIVE COACHING

ALL OF US do coach people in some form or another at different times. But taking to coaching as a profession or a natural calling is quite something else. The incidental coach may be able to pull it off sometimes but consistently achieving high levels of quality and success is what sets the executive coach apart from the rest.

Some people are better suited to take up coaching. They appear to have the natural flair and character for it. They have the right combination of attitude, traits, motivation and the will to persist. They have in them the capabilities, skills and competencies that help them craft their magic with the coachees. To them, it is a natural extension of who they are inside. Coaching as a practice is well soaked into the fabric of their being.

To the others, the coaching activity requires learning, preparation and effort. They may even experience coaching as complicated, laborious and difficult. To them, an occasional foray into the field is enough, and they do not intend to nor invest in becoming a coach at heart.

The list of competencies, capabilities and skills that could come in handy in efficient coaching can be endless. Each little one on the list can make a subtle difference in the way the coachee is able to respond to the efforts. The major and significant ones are discussed here to help understand how they can be worked with and developed.

PERSONAL COMPETENCE AND EXPERTISE

In a learning environment, there can be few things more credible than the expertise in a chosen field. So, also in the Executive Coaching environment, the expertise and established competence in any field that the coach has known interest in is definitely one of the important assets.

Coaching is a field in itself but the coach has to ideally have an area of expertise himself as the foundation for the coaching practice. The coach, having worked in some aspect of organizational functioning and having acquired a level of expertise, would go a long way in enhancing his own standing in the profession. High professional standing comes in handy when the organization seeks to associate coachees with the coach and also build a credible case for taking on the coach.

The area and genre of coaching has a direct bearing on the need for the coach having an acceptable level of expertise in the area. In skill and performance coaching, the coach has to be one with demonstrable expertise in that particular skill and having a credible track record of performance himself. This is particularly so if the coach is one from inside the organization. In coaching related to acquisition of particular technical competency by the coachees, established expertise in the area is almost a prerequisite for the coach.

It must also be said here that often the best in the field of practice does not automatically qualify as the best coach. Across the world, in the world of sport where the concept took root, or in organizational settings, it is often the practitioner who excels in work and has the requisite coaching orientation and skills that are able to morph into becoming great coaches rather than the best in the business. Perhaps the best invests so much mind space into becoming and being the best that there is little room to fit in the coaching skills and competencies needed. It is really a good option to leave the best in staying the best than saddling him with the burden of coaching. This would certainly be a good polemical issue for debate.

Now then, there is the expertise in coaching itself that has to be established for the executive coach to gain an acceptable level of credibility. Coaching is in itself a specialized field now, and while some form of certification by any certifying authority or organization does help with the uninitiated, a credible track record is often the best calling card. Knowing the intricacies and nuances in coaching well beyond the beaten path and into the nook and cranny of the practice is definitely a huge asset for the executive coach.

MATURITY AND WISDOM

The executive coach is always looked at as someone who is a substantial distance ahead of the coachee or his peers in his ability to carry the coachee to achieve greater heights. This also requires the coach to have the ability to differentiate issues, to handle and work with ambiguities and to navigate through several situations of apparent complexity and conflicts. Very often, it is the maturity of the coach in being able to keep a cool head and work through problem and issues that appear to be unsolvable and too complex to unravel that makes for any possible success in the Executive Coaching process.

Maturity has been variably defined as the ability and feel of the person to act and respond to circumstances and environment in the manner that would be appropriate without being carried away by the conflicting pulls of extraneous issues and subjects. Maturity comes with the experience of having been in or handled similar situations earlier. Then again, direct experience may also not be necessary to gain maturity if the ability and skill to conceptualize and extrapolate from limited exposure is good. Maturity also comes from learning, development of one's competencies and honing one's craft to a high degree.

The executive coach is a practitioner of his craft in the same manner of speaking. His exposure and experience in dealing with a wide array of people and issues build his maturity in the field of his practice. Long years of working with people and dedication to the practice of the profession can work well to accord him a high level of maturity. This would stand him in good stead in dealing with most forms of problems, issues and circumstances that may arise in the Executive Coaching process.

Wisdom, at the same time, is the uncanny knack of knowing what is right to be done or acted upon at the right time to obtain an optimal result. It is also the way of using knowledge, perceptions and ideas with that judicious mix. It is the tempered means of seeing paths, solutions and insights where lesser people observe none. Differentially called sagacity, it also calls for a degree of self-control to let the task and concern at hand remain central to the process instead of emotional or personal impositions.

For the executive coach, maturity and wisdom in whatever measure are prime assets. Maturity and wisdom are not something that can be learnt as a theoretical construct. It requires long years of sustained work and focus in people development and interest in seeking to understand oneself deeper and better.

AUTHENTICITY, INTEGRITY AND OBJECTIVITY

Authenticity is the degree to which one stays true to one's beliefs, faith, values, personality or character. During the course of processes in life, there are pressures that bear on the individual to deviate. At times, this comes in the form of easier paths, less troublesome or even more favourable to other callings that one may come by. But staying true and steadfast is authenticity.

To the executive coach, authenticity and being perceived to be authentic would add so much to the image he portrays and what he stands for. Authenticity in spirit and practice would contribute immensely in how the executive coach is received by not only the coachee, but also the peers and other members of the organizational community.

Integrity has more to do with the consistent fidelity to the values, principles, ideology and morality in one's approaches and practices. It has, in recent times, come to mean the extent of honesty and truthfulness espoused in one's actions. In any case, the integrity that the executive coach should stand by is in the practice and the dealing with the issues relating to the coachee. However, the executive coach should be well aware that being associated with the profession would lend to him being under watch at most times. This being so, integrity in all walks of life becomes a natural calling. This is as much a quality as it is a deliberate practice and philosophy.

The executive coach should also have the ability to rise above the issues and matters that are being dealt with and see them for what they are, without the shackles of being involved in it as such. The crucial thing here for the executive coach is to be able to retain objectivity while being in the thick of dealing with the issue at hand.

Objectivity can be journalistic in its understanding and definition or be carried to the higher levels of the philosophic. Fairness, unencumbered, non-partisan, wholly factual, devoid of opinion or bias are some of the ways to look at objectivity. These would apply well to the Executive Coaching situation. And the coach should have the ability to rise above the mundane and take a detached view of positions, circumstances and concerns. At the same time, there could also be a call on the executive coach to be able to take matters into consideration without the element of judgement of any kind, conscious or otherwise. This philosophical position of objectivity goes a long way in enhancing the credibility and faith the coachee has on the executive coach.

Objectivity comes from practice of looking at matters dispassionately and not associating emotions or individual feelings to them. The executive coach must be able to handle each issue on its merit without being swayed by any particular extraneous influence.

EMOTIONAL MATURITY

Emotional maturity is the general ability to understand, assess and be in control of emotions and circumstances leading to emotional spikes. Emotional maturity helps in keeping oneself on an even keel and not deviating into excess or emotional outbursts. This is true of positive as well as negative emotions.

This is sometimes also referred to as 'emotional intelligence' (EI). Emotional intelligence has various definitions and ways of looking at it. The theoretical framework largely looks at it as trait-based or activity-based intelligence. EI has had an ardent following in the recent years with several means of measuring it being put forth. However, what is important here is the ability of the executive coach to deal with emotions within the context of the process and the relationships that result in the process.

Critical to the success of the relationship, the process and the credibility is the capability of the executive coach to not let decisions and choices be made based on the emotional state of the moment. He should have the detachment to separate the emotional context of the issue and the substantive content of it. Keeping this 'level-headed' stand is what makes for the trust the coachee will be able to invest in the coach. Being able to rise above the emotional waves that are normal to any dynamic relationship is valued often. The coach should be able to take this stand even with the clear understanding and recognition of the emotions from either side.

In some circumstances, there is the possibility of encountering apparently contradictory emotional states, not just in oneself, but also in the context of dealing with other people. Maturity calls for dealing with or coping with these emotional contradictions.

ISSUE IDENTIFICATION AND DIAGNOSTIC SKILLS

Executive Coaching revolves around resolving issues and helping coachee develop in the direction he has chosen. Sometimes development is itself the issue. Therefore, the ability of the coach to identify and clearly delineate the issues and work out a strategy to handle, resolve and manage the issue becomes critical.

It is in this light that the ability of the coach in spotting the issue amongst the clutter gains importance. The skill is in working closely with the coachee to help him bring out the issues that may, at times, be buried deep or unidentified for long period of time and be at the root of the learning and development process.

Closely tied to this is diagnostic skill. The ability to work out a cause and effect relationship between the symptoms and the underlying causative agents is diagnostic skill. Diagnostic skill takes the ability to identify issues to the next level of specialization in the executive coach. Working in tandem, issue identification and diagnosis help the coachee understand the substance in what he may need to work with during the process.

Key components of this skill pair is in developing the innate ability to explore, to seek out the linkages in what is being presented and being able to notice patterns. It also involves the ability to ferret out the hidden or unseen threads that lead to the kernel of the issue. There is also the need to hone the ability to catch the unsaid and notice the unseen in dealing using this almost detective-like ability.

Putting the data thus gathered and to draw the right inference is the diagnostic part of the ability. Here, the crucial component of the skill is to perceive pattern and connections where none may be apparent at the outset. The ability to relate known knowledge and data to extrapolations of the possible with a grounding to reality comes into play here. Diagnostic skill also carries with it the temperance to not be alarmist in approach. While the skill is invaluable in areas like medicine, technology, etc., in the Executive Coaching field, it is just as highly regarded as an essential skill.

EMPATHY AND SENSITIVITY

Empathy is the ability to put oneself in the other person's position and see things as the other person would. It is the ability to look beyond one's own preoccupations and enter the world of the other. This puts the other at comfort of knowing well that he is understood as he stands, without the burden of justification or judgement. It also works well to establish a stronger relationship between the two. Empathy is effectually the basis for good and enduring relationship. This would, at the very outset, be an essential ability in the executive coach.

Empathizing requires the coach to know well the coachee in the coachee's own terms. The ability calls for being able to hold a wide array of interests; being exposed to different aspects of people's nature; having a deep insight into and understanding a variety of intertwined feelings and emotions in relationships; having experienced a wide range of situations and circumstances to understand how people react to them; are some of the factors that help build a good ability to empathize with others.

While empathy is understanding and getting an appreciation of the situation of others, it does not reflect being in agreement with them. Empathy often faces the difficulty of differentiating from sympathy. Sympathy has a sense of agreement and alignment with the emotive and feeling level concerns of the other. Empathy, on the other hand, stays with understanding and figuring out the position and consideration of the other, leaving the matter of what to do with the understanding as an issue of choice. The differentiation is important as often the coachee expects sympathy, and on being accorded empathy, the responses may express being let down by the coach.

Sensitivity refers to the ability of the executive coach to be able to perceive and gather the emotions, feelings and, in some form, the thoughts of the coachee, even without them being articulated. Sensitivity heightens the ability to perceive those that may not be apparent to the common eye. This requires the individual to have a high level of self-awareness before he may be able to rise to the level of awareness of others. This also requires a close feel for the other and an investment in the intensity of association.

For the executive coach, having the ability to empathize and the sensitivity to perceive more than that is apparent with the coachee gives him a definite advantage in helping the coachee develop greater self-awareness and progress faster in the chosen path of development.

COMMUNICATION BASKET

Communication skill is not a single skill, but a collection of related skills involved in transaction of information and messages with the outside world. This involves the ability to translate ideas and thoughts with sufficient clarity into messages, packaging messages for the right media chosen, understanding the connected receivers, making provision for feedback, to receive and give feedback appropriately, to listen in suitable ways, to understand the usages of different formats and forms of communication, etc. It is one agglomeration of several skills packaged into apparently one single entity.

For the executive coach, the communication capability is perhaps on top of the list of essential capabilities and competencies. Beginning with the ideation process to the other end of handling receipt of communication, it is a long arrangement of distinct competencies.

Capturing the idea fully and with consistent clarity is needed for the coach to be able to handle and transact with ease and alacrity the expertise that he has in other aspects of the coaching process. Then on, the translation of the idea into forms that can be received by someone like the coachee is just as important. The easier this happens seamlessly, the more comfortable the coach will find himself handling the communication process. Understanding the frame of reference and the communication capability profile of the coachee makes for customizing the executive coach's communication to the specific requirement of the coachee.

Taking this further, the capability of the coach in both verbal and transverbal—paraverbal and nonverbal—will come to be tested under all sort of circumstances during the coaching process.

Particularly in Executive Coaching, the subtleties in the transaction become critical since the dealings between the coach and the coachee become more complex and with stress sometimes queering the pitch. The nuances in verbal, paraverbal and nonverbal inflections and cues come into play when the issues tend to heat up during transactions in delicate or sensitive matters. It will do the coach a world of good to be highly proficient in catching, interpreting and analyzing these fine and subtle cues. He should also ideally be very skilled in using them.

In the verbal communication component of communication, the role of language is significant. In this, the capability of the executive coach in handling the language of currency is of importance. Ideal would be to seek to understand and transact in the language in which the coachee is comfortable. The language aspect includes the proficiency with vocabulary, the command and control and construction of meaning using the language. The higher the familiarity with the level and usage of language understood and used by the coachee—in terms of the dialect, slang, clichés, metaphors and examples—the better the communication is likely to be.

There is also the huge area of paraverbal and nonverbal aspects of communication. This being closely linked to the cultural context of communication, the executive coach will have to work at plugging in to the needs of understanding and decoding them. It requires the executive coach to study the nuances of the paraverbal and nonverbal expressions in the repertoire used by the coachee. Paraverbal, riding on the verbal component, are the non-language components of the spoken words, like: accent, intonation, emphasis, gesture supplements to the spoken words, etc. They play a very significant part in decoding the language to catch the subtleties of shift in meaning.

The nonverbal aspects encompass the huge swath of transaction of meaning in non-language–based messages. They include kinesics (popularly called body language), space, time, colour, graphics, social codes, dress, adornments, etc. This forms the significantly major part of any transaction of communication taking place in all settings. It is closely bound to culture, situation and context of the transaction. It constitutes as much as 95 per cent of the transaction and so understanding and knowing them intimately is an essential requirement for high level of proficiency in communication.

Then again, the capability of the coach in using different media and the numerous formats they come in would be a great asset to consider having in the quiver. Not that all or most may be needed all the time; it would auqur well to have a good capability in them anyway.

While interpersonal tête-à-tête spoken medium is often the one most employed, other media will also certainly come into play at various times. Most people would consider proficiency in spoken medium adequate to qualify as skilled, but it is only one aspect of communication. The executive coach's capability in the written medium is almost as critical. There is an even chance that crucial communication will be transacted in this medium several times during the process.

Then again, there is the currently popular issue in communication of ability of the executive coach to adapt to the technology intervening in the communication process. Even in the spoken format, as in others, the presence of technological interfaces brings with it the issue of being able to understand, operate and learn the language that the technology brings with it. For instance, the ubiquitous mobile communication technology has introduced the language used in speaking on mobile phones that is decidedly different from the direct tête-à-tête conversation. Also, the language of texting is so much different from either the conventional written or spoken communication. The executive coach can, in no way, be exempt from adapting to such changes washing over the communication space. He has to plug in or be left out as there is no saying what the preference of the coachee would be and his opinion of the coach who is not comparably savvy as he in the use of the technology.

The other critical component in the communication basket is listening skill. Listening is not a passive activity in the communication process and requires specific capability to excel in. This is one aspect that the executive coach cannot afford to ignore or diminish the importance of. Listening is an active communication activity and it involves participation in the communication process with complete involvement in the transactions taking place. Active listening entails interacting with the speaker with transactions reciprocating the speaker's communication without either taking over or denigrating the speaker's role in the process. Active listening enhances the enthusiasm of the speaker to carry forth better and increases the value of communication.

Carrying this further, the executive coach should be able to move into the realms of empathetic listening for boosting his effectiveness in the coaching process. Empathetic listening takes the listening process to the next higher level of going beyond the spoken or tangible transaction and catches the nuances of the unspoken or hidden aspect of the communication as well. This delves deeper within to reach the underlying feelings and emotions of the speaker that may, at times, remain untransacted due to the incapability of the speaker.

Communication also involves the transaction of feedback. This requires a different handling of the process due to the very nature of the content. Here, the uniqueness of it is manifested in the manner in which the communication is packaged. Deciding and arranging the ambience and environment of communication, preparing the recipient, organizing the process, designing the messages appropriately, choosing the right medium to deliver sensitive feedback, preparing on the follow-up stages of the feedback, preparation to receive and accept feedback, etc., makes for the entire process being distinct from other forms of communication transaction. There is definitely going to be several instances of feedback needing to be transacted during the Executive Coaching process. This requires the executive coach to be well-versed in handling this aspect of communication with ease and alacrity.

Just as important in the communication skills basket is the ability of the executive coach to enthuse and evoke the coachee to communicate openly and freely in the coaching process and environment. This requires the coach to be able to inspire the coachee to express and receive communication with comfort and acceptance.

FACILITATION SKILLS

Facilitation refers to the function of providing assistance in activity of some form. In the case of Executive Coaching, the facilitation skill in the coach is the ability to help the coachee arrive at understanding and agreements in areas he finds difficult to deal with.

This may, for the most part, be true in the case of some sections of people and issues of particular kinds, which the coachee has trouble in handling. The executive coach may work as a mediator or intervening factor to help work through the rough patches without being directly involved or taking over control from the coachee. This is principally intended as a learning exercise and not as a proxy or negotiator on the coachee's behalf.

Facilitation skill requires a good understanding of the dynamics of the environment, knowing the situation and positions being taken by the people involved, an ability to deal with people of different kinds, capacity to build and maintain functional relationships with a variety of people and good communication capability. In the case of the executive coach, the orientation to convert facilitation events into learning opportunities is definitely an added asset.

CONFLICT MANAGEMENT AND RESOLUTION SKILLS

Conflicts are inevitable. These do surface often in circumstances where there is any form of interactions between people. Differences, disagreements and disputes are different manifestations of conflict. The key is not in denial, but resolution or management of conflict that relationships thrive on. The skill is in achieving a good measure of this. This is also critical for the executive coach, as more often than otherwise he is in the midst of conflicts and contradictions, and it is his calling to work past these.

Skill in conflict resolution and management encompasses the ability to understand the nature of conflicts, the various manifestations and ramifications of it, the causes of the conflict and the impact and result of it on the people and circumstances. The ability to understand the way people react to conflict and particularly how the coachee reacts to it is an added talent for the executive coach.

Not all conflicts are unpleasant and unnecessary. There are enormous benefits to be had from conflicts too. Being able to gauge the positive uses of conflicts helps in its resolution and prevents its escalation into unmanageable proportions. The executive coach has the brief of not only navigating through conflicts that may afflict the relationship and the intervention, but also to help the coachee imbibe the skill too. Variably, the executive coach will have to play the roles of peacemaker, peacekeeper or peace broker.

RELATIONSHIP SKILLS

Relationship skill has to do with the ability to establish, maintain and carry forward healthy functioning relationships with people. The wider the variety of people involved, the more complex and, therefore, the more difficult the skill. It could also become more complex when dealing with people with relationship disabilities themselves.

The skill involves understanding the person being invited into the relationship to begin with, and the tenor and nature of the relationship. The critical thing that needs also to be understood is that the relationship itself becomes an entity that comes into being at the instance of association and has demands of its own in the process. From there begins the dynamics of the process. The skill is also to read and stay ahead of the process.

The skill calls for knowing the balances in the relationships and keeping them on an even keel. The balance from either side—of needs in and from the relationship, the contributions that nurture and maintain it, the actions and distractions that wound and diminish the strengths of it, the takeaways and extractions from it and the investments into the future of it—is critical for the relationship to move forward. In this sense, the skill is also to be able to discern the opportunities to carry the relationship to positions of greater strength, to pre-empt, resolve and manage conflicts and discords that may arise between the relationship partners and the create the mutuality to maximize and harness the synergy that grows in the relationship.

Any relationship is a shared enterprise and therefore, however unequal, there still is mutuality in its existence and process. The skill here also encompasses the balance of skill requirements within the relationship, complementing each other where required. Further down, good housekeeping is as important a need as anything else in the growth and development of good relationships. The skill is to manage this as well.

In the case of the executive coach, there is often a higher burden of working the relationship, particularly in the initial phases, on the coach. As the process proceeds, one of the spin-offs and takeaways from the Executive Coaching process itself would be better relationship skills imbibed from the coach.

REFERRAL SKILLS

Often not wholly identified as a skill, referral is more practised in clinical medicine as a distinct practice than in management science. Although, it should be said that there is almost as much of the practice taking place without being identified as such, without it being accorded the formal recognition.

Referral is the practice of personally recommending someone to another practitioner for better or more specialized care. The skill comes in the exercise of the discretionary element in the process. The key aspect is in discerning whether the individual needs to be referred to someone else more specialized in the practice or not. The critical factor extends into working out when the action needs to be taken and also the appropriate means of extending the referral to the individual himself.

Then it is the issue of working out the appropriate practitioner and then the right combination in the best interest of the individual being referred. Its skill is also to work out the brief that would help the specialist being referred to work out a better line of care. Referral is not an abdication of work, responsibility or accountability. It is much more in enlisting the aid of someone who can deliver better results under the circumstance. There is, in addition, the matter of follow-up in the process as well that needs to be undertaken.

Carry this into the world of Executive Coaching and it devolves onto the coach to work out if, for that particular issue and development need of the coachee, would the coach himself be the best person to work with or would it do the coachee better if the aid of someone more specialized in that particular area be enlisted. Here, the diagnosis of the issues and discerning of the core aspect of concern is important.

This becomes important where there are matters of mental health, physical well-being, technical specializations, psychological issues, organizational concerns or, at times, ethical concerns involved. While the executive coach does have to take the call on the matter of taking the referral option, it is ideally done with consultation and consent of the coachee. The skill is to become aware of the need at the right time, to determine the need to go in for the option and then working out the downstream process.

It is neither an easy skill to develop nor is it simple to practise. But having this in the repertoire of skills would be a definite asset when the issues become more complicated and the difficulties with the coaching process become more thorny. This is, in that sense, really a high-end skill for the executive coach.

NEGOTIATION AND PERSUASION SKILLS

Not all coaches come in enamoured with the process, prospects or the protagonist. Many times the executive coach has to work his way through reluctance with suave and deft persuasion. There could also be times where the dealings with the coachee, the environment and other stakeholders may be contentious but crucial enough for some form of negotiated solution to be warranted. It in is these circumstances that the capability of the executive coach in negotiation and persuasion will be tested.

The skill in negotiation is to be able to understand the situations well, the dynamics of interaction and interface between the parties involved, the stakes being invested and expected realization from them, the relative positions and flexibility that can be expected and minimum configuration of viable solutions in the quandary. Keeping these in mind, the ability to work through any form of creative solutions is the desired goal.

In most circumstances, there is the possibility of any or more parties involved being inflexible, stubborn or unyielding. In these cases, the expectation would be to figure some permutation or combination what would make them see the advantage of agreement over the contrary position. There could be the need to apply any form of persuasion, for example: selling, influencing, cajoling, convincing, pleading or negotiating some trade-off or even coercion.

In the context of the Executive Coaching scenario, the negotiation and persuasion take the form of the coach having to work out viable and acceptable context for the intervention, working out the setting and terms with the HR of the organization, getting the coachee to understand and accept the framework of executive coaching, getting the coachee to see the issues being worked with, work out solutions if the process gets stalled sometimes, working out the path to move forward towards the close of the process, etc. With the confidence borne out of having the skills to stay one step ahead and to see the process through in most situations of difficulty will help the executive coach work freely in the intervention.

COUNSELLING SKILLS

Counselling is the ability to help individuals find solutions and resolutions to the difficulties and issues that they confront. The skill to perform such an activity involves many of the skills and competencies discussed earlier. It involves understanding the person and the issue, the nature of the problem, the ability of the person to seek and arrive at possible solution or resolution, the ability of the person to articulate and then walking the individual through the process and follow-up.

The process begins with exploration, leading to diagnosis of the issue, helping articulate and seek solutions, working out the action steps and then onto the follow-up. These are the essential broad steps in the process. The ability is to keep with the need for helping the individual through the counselling process. The counsellor should have the skill in reading the needs of the individual, help him articulate and isolate the issue or problem from mental clutter and work towards clarity of thought. Application of related skills of communication, empathy, sensitivity, facilitation, etc., in the counselling context comes into play here too.

The important aspect of counselling is that the counsellor is not the solution provider but a facilitator or helper in seeking and working with the individual's own solutions. In Executive Coaching, the coach may find himself in situations where he would have to play the role of a counsellor where there is a need for the coachee to develop his own ability to seek solutions rather than work with one provided. The executive coach should also have the ability to judge when the situation warrants the counselling approach to be adapted.

6. EXECUTIVE COACHING TOOLS

THE EXECUTIVE COACH has, as a part of helping the coachee in the learning and development pursuit, to understand and facilitate the coachee's understanding of himself in various facets. There are several tools and instruments available to the coach in this task. These are intended to inventory the traits, personality and other features to complement the coach's own reading of the coachee.

The executive coach has a quiver full of arrows that he carries. Not that each one will be used or that each one will find its exact mark or serve its assigned purpose—but knowing the repertoire of implements available and knowing their utility would make the executive coach a craftsman on top of his art.

There are many tools and instruments available to the executive coach. They range in utility and need in assessing the coachee, calibrating various aspects and, in some cases, assisting in diagnosis. The list of tools discussed here are by no means exhaustive, but the popular and oft used ones are here to give a perspective on the array existing. The list of tools mentioned here are for what they are, their background and genesis to help understand them and their intended purpose. The discussion and indicator mentioned here are in the nature of an introduction to the instrument and indicative of the kind of use they can be put to. It is not intended to be the source or tutor for the use of the instrument. The discussion provides a direction, suggestion of when and how they can be used, broadly what they indicate and the purpose they may serve to the executive coach and to the coachee.

While extreme caution is advised in working out the choice of the instrument to be used, care must be taken to ensure optimal utilization of the benefits from using the instrument itself. Further, all or most of the instruments and tools require a level of expertise in their administration and are not intended for lay use.

Most are patented or copyrighted and therefore requisite permission would be necessary for their use.

These are the tools executive coaches have been using over the years and most have stood the test of time and have also evolved in their sharpness and specialization.

THE LEARNING STYLE INVENTORY

The Learning Style Inventory is designed following the Learning Styles Model developed by David A. Kolb. Assessing the learning style helps determine the best approach for the individual in learning. It also indicates the individuals preferred learning style and therefore provides a foundation for interacting with the individual in a learning environment. For the executive coach, this can serve as a basis for working out learning strategies in case of extended learning sessions with the coachee. This would also give the individual an opportunity in participating in the decision regarding the choice of learning style.

David Kolb's Learning Styles Model was based on the experiential learning theory. This theory explains the approached towards capturing and deriving learning from experiences and the approaches towards transforming and configuring these experiences. The two related approaches in capturing experiences are 'Concrete Experience' and 'Abstract Conceptualisation'; and the related approaches to transforming experiences are 'Reflective Observation' and 'Active Experimentation'.

Kolb suggests that a good learning process involves the individual with all the four modes in response the calling in different situations. This ensures effective learning experience for the individual. However, as individuals attempt to develop their learning faculties in response to encountered experiences, they tend to strengthen one of the capturing and one of the transforming approaches in preference over the other. The resulting combination creates the individuals own characteristic learning style and preference. In combination, the learning style may be:

1. Converger
2. Diverger
3. Assimilator
4. Accommodator

Convergers have a preference for Abstract Conceptualization and Active Experimentation approaches. They tend to be good at deductive reasoning in problem solving and arriving at the practicability of ideas in application. Divergers on the other hand prefer the Concrete Experience and Reflective Observation approaches to learning. They are good at seeing the issues and problems from different perspectives and, being imaginative, come up with ideas.

Assimilators prefer Abstract Conceptualization and Reflective Observation approaches. They are capable of working out theoretical models using inductive reasoning. The Accommodators prefer Concrete Experience and Active Experimentation approaches. They are hands-on kind of people with taste for actually getting into doing things instead of theorizing and studying.

Kolb's model has been the set around which the Learning Styles Inventory was built. The individual's relative preference for any of the four styles can be worked out through this inventory.

Peter Honey and Alan Mumford adapted the David Kolb's model to the managerial experience and the calling of problem solving and decision-making. They proposed a four-stage cycle:

1. Having an experience
2. Reviewing the experience
3. Concluding from the experience
4. Planning the next step

The learning styles were aligned to the stages in the cycle and were named Activist, Reflector, Theorist and Pragmatist. Unlike personality traits or characteristics, these were preferred choices made either consciously or by the circumstances the individual found himself in. The Honey and Mumford Learning Styles Questionnaire, unlike the Kolb Learning Style Inventory, is more direct in its approach. It works directly with the individual's preference to learn. Using this, the individual is encouraged to recognize the potential in the learning preferred approach and also work at strengthening the underutilized approaches to help with an all-round approach to learning.

THE JOHARI WINDOW

Joseph Luft and Harry Ingham, in 1955, created a cognitive psychological tool called the Johari Window (Figure 6.1). The name was derived from the first part of their first names. The Johari Window is useful in helping people understand their interpersonal relationships and communication.

Figure 6.1: The Johari Window

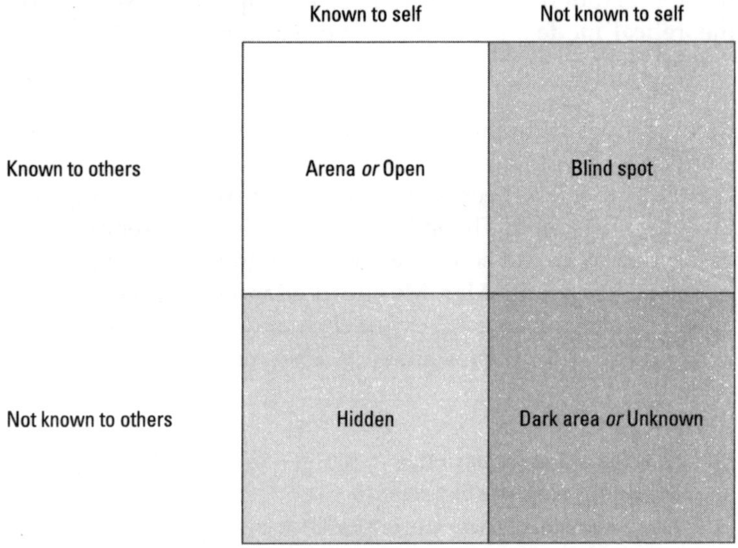

	Known to self	Not known to self
Known to others	Arena or Open	Blind spot
Not known to others	Hidden	Dark area or Unknown

The Johari Window concept works around how an individual perceives self and how others perceive the individual. The similarities and differences help understand how each individual deals with interrelationship with the outside world.

The four panes in the window deal with the four quadrants of perception. The 'Open' or the 'Arena' quadrant or pane represents the part of the individual known to the individual and to others. The 'Hidden' pane is that personal space kept by the individual to himself and not shared with others. The third pane, 'Blind Spot', is the part of the individual that he is not aware of, but is known to others. And the 'Dark Area' or the 'Unknown' is the part of the individual unknown both to others and to the individual himself.

In the exercise using Johari Window, the individual and a group, his peers, are given a list of 55 adjectives. They are asked to pick five or six of them which best describe the individual's personality. These chosen adjectives are used to build a map of the perceived personality profile of the individual.

The adjectives chosen by both the individual and the peers are placed in the 'Open' quadrant representing traits that everybody is aware of about the individual. The adjectives chosen only by the individual and not by the peers are placed in the 'Hidden' quadrant—the personal space. The adjectives chosen only by the peers are the traits that fall in the 'Blind Spot' area. These are traits that the individual is unaware of about himself. And the rest of the adjectives are placed in the 'Dark Area' or the 'Unknown' quadrant. This set may also contain traits that may not apply or because of the collective ignorance of their applicability to the individual.

The Johari Window is useful in small group sessions when there is sufficient openness to discuss personalities and accept candid comments. While the collection of adjectives is generally positive, an inverse version, often called the 'Nohari Window', carries adjectives showing negative traits.

THE DISC PROFILE

The DISC profile is a popular assessment tool in profiling the personality of executives and managers in their workplace performance orientation and related attitudinal aspects. DISC is an acronym for the four indicators scaled by the instrument: Dominance, Influence, Steadiness and Conscientiousness. It is a group of psychological inventories based on the work of William Moulton Marston, Micheal Landrup and Walter Clarke. John G. Grier invented the DISC assessment.

Dominance relates to power, control and assertiveness expressed in performance and interactional dynamics. Influence relates to social situation and communication while Steadiness looks at patience, thoughtfulness and persistence (also called Submission in Marston's time). Conscientiousness (or Caution or Compliance—in Marston's time) relates to structure and organization.

While *D* and *I* are considered to represent the extraverted aspects, *C* and *S* represent the introverted aspects of the personality. The four dimensions can be grouped into a grid with the vertical dimension representing the factor of being assertive or passive while the open versus guarded aspect is on the horizontal in the matrix.

High score in the intensity of *D* is interpreted as being very active on dealing with problems and challenges while low *D* score points towards people wanting to be more thorough and consider more issues and factors before committing to a decision. High Score on *D* is also indicative of people being more forceful, egocentric, determined, aggressive, demanding, strong-willed, etc. Conservative, cautious, mild, modest, amicable, pacific are the words applied to low-*D*-score people.

High-*I*-score people tend to be more emotional in the way that they approach persuasion and influence with emotive and feeling level talk and activity being the preferred path. They are usually seen as warm, enthusiastic, magnetic, demonstrative, optimistic, kind and considerate. The low-*I*-score people are often described as calculating, logical, detached, pessimistic, sceptical, critical or suspicious with them preferring data, facts and information doing their persuasion for them.

High-*S*-score people prefer steady and stable environment with low threshold for change and sudden variance. They tend to be seen as calm, predictable, stable, consistent, relaxed, deliberate, less expressive, etc. The low-*S*-score people like variance and change and are often described as restless, impatient, eager, impulsive and spontaneous at times.

Adherence to rules, regulations, procedures, precedence, structures and systems is the hallmark of high *C* score. They like being precise and as near perfection as possible—the first time and each time. They tend to be neat, systematic, accurate, diplomatic, tactful, careful and cautious. Those with low *C* score prefer the independence of not conforming. They challenge rules and set norms, and more often are seen as stubborn, self-willed, unsystematic, opinionated and, at times, arbitrary.

DISC is quite popular in corporate as an assessment and indicative tool to help executives understand themselves and take appropriate measures in self-development. This is a valuable tool in assisted self-development as well.

THE MYERS BRIGGS TYPE INDICATOR (MBTI)

Katherine Cook Briggs and her daughter Isabel Briggs Myer created the 'Briggs Myer Type Indicator' in 1942. The name was changed to 'Myer Briggs Type Indicator' in 1956. It is a psychometric questionnaire designed to measure psychological preferences in how people perceive the world and make decisions.

Briggs's basic idea of personality types originated from her observation and study of the marked differences she saw in the personalities of her future son-in-law and other members of the family. She further developed the idea working closely along the personality types described by Carl Jung. Myers further added to her mother's research in later years.

One of the most widely used personality tests in organizations, the MBTI works with a questionnaire that takes around 20 minutes for the subject to answer. On analysis, the subject is provided a precise and directed description of his personality type based on four bi-polar dimensions:

- Introversion–Extraversion (I–E): Derives his energy and drive from being with people (E), or, in being solitary and from within (I).
- Intuition–Sensing (N–S): Garners information directly from data and facts around (S), or, indirectly through understanding of relationships and possibilities (N).
- Feeling–Thinking (F–T): Arriving at decisions through objective logic (T), or, through subjective feelings (F).
- Perceiving–Judging (P–J): Likes to be systematic in planning and organizing to know what is to be expected (J), or, likes to leave things more open to options and being flexible (P).

From these four categories, the 16 personality types have been derived by combination (Box 6.1): each of the personality type has been described in detail.

Box 6.1: The Myers Briggs Type Indicator Personality Types

ISTJ	ISFJ	INFJ	INTJ
ISTP	ISFP	INFP	INTP
ESTP	ESFP	ENFP	ENTP
ESTJ	ESFJ	ENFJ	ENTJ

While the description of each of the personality types has been found to be accurate by any measure, the issue has been of the mutual exclusivity of each of the types. The personality classification is to be clearly stated as a type and not as a trait. The MBTI classifies the type of personality and not the strength of the preference or the ability indicated. Unlike the trait-based questionnaire like the 16PF, the MBTI does not define the clear preference of one or the other choice in the questionnaire and does not calibrate the extent of preference of one in comparison with the other.

The MBTI insists that the individual is the best judge of the fit of his own personality type. There is also no claim to one type being better than the others or any being the best. The questionnaire also does not indicate any preference as being right or wrong as such. The administration of the questionnaire is mandated to be voluntary and with an assurance of confidentiality of the results and interpretation. There is also the need for effective feedback and explanation to be accompanied with the administration of the test. The MBTI is still an indicative and not a conclusive calibration of the personality types, especially as the questionnaire is user scored.

In spite of the abundant caution and ethical barriers in place along with the attempt at imposing strict copyright codes around the use of the questionnaire, it continues to be as loosely used as its popularity increases in organizations and L&D set up around the world.

There is the issue often faced of using the MBTI as a factor in selection or placement, in spite of warnings against such use. This has lead to subjects faking their responses to suit the immediate needs, defeating the very purpose of the instrument. Then again, there is often the case of people finding themselves constrained by the definition and classification dealt out to them after taking the questionnaire. They find themselves trying to behave and be as they have been defined by the instrument rather than being their natural self, which may be different.

With executive coaches skilled and trained in the use of the instrument, it is certainly a powerful tool in understanding the personality type of the coachee and planning the best fit for him in the scheme of things. The coach could also provide valuable support in interpreting the indications and the type for the coachee and thus help him know himself better.

THE 16PF QUESTIONNAIRE

The Sixteen Personality Factor (16PF) Questionnaire is a multivariant questionnaire developed by psychologist Raymond B. Cattell and his associates after decades of research. The questionnaire looks at describing the personality of individuals based on self-reported traits, inclinations, perspectives and behaviours.

The questionnaire has undergone many iterations and editions over the years and the current editions contains about 185 multiple choice items for the individual to deal with. This has a paper and pencil version and the computer-assisted one as well.

Raymond Cattell, in 1946, used a factor analysis technique with the emerging technology of computing to examine the Alport–Odbert list of personality describing words. He reordered the almost 18,000 words into 181 clusters and generated 12 factors that he felt determined the description of personality. To the 12, he added four more that he thought should have figured in the list.

The list is comprehensive in its inclusion. The list: Warmth, Reasoning, Emotional Stability, Dominance, Liveliness, Rule Consciousness, Social Boldness, Sensitivity, Vigilance, Abstractedness, Privateness, Apprehension, Openness to Change, Self reliance, Perfectionism, Tension.

With these 16 factors as the basis, Cattell constructed the 16PF questionnaire. This has, over time, been used by corporate and other organizations in assessing the personalities of people within the organization and also the potential employees. Research in later years had not been able to replicate with reasonable accuracy the claims of Cattell. Although accusations of having retained too many factors had come up, Raymond Cattell's 16PF remains one of the popular personality assessment questionnaires.

THE FIRO-B

William Schutz had been the contemporary of the likes of Abraham Maslow and Carl Rogers. He taught at several universities in the USA and has been the pioneer in some of the far-reaching techniques in understanding human behaviour and psychology.

In 1958, he introduced the interpersonal relationship theory called the Fundamental Interpersonal Relationship Orientation (FIRO). This theory explained the dynamics and the underworld of small groups. The theory works on the belief that when in groups, people look to fulfil three main interpersonal needs— Affection or Openness, Control and Inclusion.

The Schutz self-scoring instrument looks to calibrate how the individual feels in groups with respect to the three needs in two aspects. The 'expressed' aspect is the way the individual behaves or expresses his needs of inclusion, control or openness; and the 'wanted' aspect looks at the desire of the individual to be treated in particular ways by others on the three needs.

The self-reporting FIRO-B questionnaire helps measure the extent and intensity of interaction a person wants in these six areas—Expressed Inclusion (EI), Expressed Control (EC), Expressed Affection (EA), Wanted Inclusion (WI), Wanted Control (WC) and Wanted Affection (WA). Shutz created the questionnaire as a measuring instrument that has six scales of nine-item questions.

For each area of interpersonal needs, the FIRO-B indicates three types of behaviour that would be evident: excessive, ideal or deficient. Excessive is when the individual invests heavily and consistently into satisfying the need he feels in that aspect of the interpersonal interaction with the group. Deficient is when the individual does not directly try or manoeuvre to satisfy the need. Ideal refers to the balance where the need is satisfied.

Using this, Schutz identified the following types. In Inclusion aspect: *(a)* the Undersocial (with low EI and low WI scores); *(b)* the Social (with moderate EI and moderate WI scores); and *(c)* the Oversocial (with high EI and high WI scores). In Control aspect: *(a)* the Abdicrat (with low EC and low WC scores); *(b)* Democrat (with moderate EC and moderate WC scores); and *(c)* the Autocrat (with high EC and high WC scores). In Affection or Openness aspect: *(a)* the Underpersonal (with low EA and low WA scores); *(b)* the Personal (with moderate EA and moderate WA scores); and *(c)* the Overpersonal (with high EA and high WA scores).

All the six scores, though computed independently from the questionnaire, tend to be interconnected and interpretation of the meaning and indications presented by the permutation and patterns of the scores is critical. Experience and width of exposure of the expert interpreting the scores is a vital factor in the accuracy and validity of the interpretation.

FIRO-B is a popular and widely used instrument. While the scores are not static and may be subject to change over time, it is an excellent basis for understanding the interpersonal orientation of the coachee and plan forward from there.

Developing further on the FIRO theory, Schutz has advanced the instrument to measure more and newer aspects of interpersonal relationships in groups—FIRO Element-B: Behaviour; FIRO Element-F: Feelings; FIRO Element-W: Work relationships; FIRO Element-O: Organizational climate; FIRO Element-C: Close relationships; and FIRO Element-P: Parental relationships. These are collectively called Elements of Awareness.

THE BELBIN TEAM ROLES INVENTORY

Developed by Meredith Belbin after study of numerous teams while at Henley Management College, the Belbin Self-perception Inventory or the Belbin Team Roles Inventory is an assessment tool used to understand an individual's innate behavioural inclination in a team environment.

The Belbin Team Roles Inventory looks at assessing how the individual behaves in a team setting and work environment. It is a behavioural tool indicating an assessed behavioural type and in not a psychometric instrument. Hence, it has to be put to use as such. Behaviour is subject to change and so also indications from the tool thereof.

The complete inventory instrument includes a 360-degree feedback from observers as well as a self-assessment questionnaire scoring how strongly the individual expresses traits from the different team roles delineated by Belbin. The assessment also helps identify how the individual may concur or differ in perceptions from that of the observers or colleagues who gave the feedback in terms of behaviour exhibited.

Belbin asserts that the team roles are not personality types and an individual may exhibit propensity towards multiple team roles. Belbin categorizes eight roles with one additional role, which may be played by any in addition to the one already being played. Four of these roles are inward looking and four are outward looking in the team context. These roles contribute to the completions of the team and facilitate the functioning of the team. Each role has strengths contributing positively and also 'allowable' weakness.

'Plant' is the role played by those in the team with inclination towards the unconventional and the unorthodox, and the creative generation of ideas. They, however, are not adept at networking and communicating within the team and have a hard time getting their ideas across to the others. The 'Resource Investigator' role in the team on the other hand sources ideas and energy from outside for the benefit of the team. While good at networking and getting ideas, the 'Resource Investigator' is not well inclined to carry the project and work to its logical conclusion, losing momentum and interest towards the end.

The 'Coordinator' role is that of a leader by default. The 'Coordinator' is able to assign, delegate and get the right people in the team to take on and be involved in the right task based on capabilities. He is able to do little else but this in the team, leaving him open to criticism and accusation of being a burden on the team. The 'Shaper' role is task-focused too, but with the intensity and the drive to get people to focus on the goals of the team. The 'Shaper' may sometimes be too aggressive for the liking of the other members of the team.

The task of working objectively and without bias on the choices and options open in the team is done by the 'Monitor Evaluator' role helping the team to arrive at logical decisions. However, they may tend to be excessively critical, putting off others and being unable to inspire others to take on tasks within the team. The 'Teamworker' role is the glue that holds the team together and lubricates the frictional synapses between the members of the team. Being a good listener and diplomat, he is able to smooth over conflicts and differences within the team. The 'Teamworker', however, is unable to act decisively in crises and tight situations.

The 'Implementor' role is the action person in the team. He is able to take on the ideas and suggestions of other members of the team and convert them into action and actionable plans. The 'Implementor' tends to be self-disciplined and efficient, but being driven by the belief in the effectiveness of his plans is unable to deviate from them and could face the criticism of being close-minded and inflexible at times. Attention to detail is the hallmark of the 'Completer Finisher' role in the team. He is able to take on the task of ensuring accuracy of operation and has a high standard set for himself and others in the quality of output in tasks. The 'Completer Finisher' tends to fret on small details, often refusing to delegate tasks and not trusting others to perform to the level of perfection. Being a perfectionist, the 'Completer Finisher' could turn out to be frustrating for others.

The common role defined by Belbin is the 'Specialist'. This could be taken on by any of the others in addition to the one being played by them in the team at the time. The 'Specialist' tends to be very knowledgeable in the specific field and will be happy to share the knowledge and wisdom with any other and the team. He is passionate about learning and looking for opportunities to find new things out. However, they tend to be confined to the narrow space of their interest and knowledge and uninterested in anything that lies outside the silo.

Belbin's team roles have particular affinities and compatibility with other roles within the team and also have repulsive effect on some of the roles. The dynamics of the team are the result of this attractions and aversions. The chemistry of attraction and repulsion helps the individual understand the interrelationships within the teams he functions in and also the impact he has on the other members of the team as a result of his preference and propensity to take on particular roles within the team. Getting an understanding of the preferred roles that the coachee often gravitates towards will help the coach prepare and guide the coachee to adapt and work the best out of being a part of any team.

THE REDDIN'S 3D LEADERSHIP MODEL

Professor W. J. Reddin's integration of what he called the 'situation demands' into leadership styles introduced the 3D theory. The 3D theory was influenced by and borrows heavily from Professor Douglas MacGregor's 'Theory X and Theory Y'. This influence was principally during the time spent by Reddin at the Massachusetts Institute of Technology. This led to his extending 'Theory X and Theory Y' into a third dimension.

He devised a simple method of measuring the leadership style use propensity on the scale of task orientation, people orientation and effectiveness in 'situation appropriateness'. Reddin thus derives eight styles — four effective or functional and four less effective or dysfunctional. Based on the grid of high or low orientation on the scales of task or people/relationship preference, Reddin worked out the dysfunctional or less effective styles of 'Deserter', 'Autocrat', 'Missionary' and 'Compromiser'. The effective or functional styles are 'Bureaucrat', 'Benign autocrat', 'Developer' and the 'Executive' styles.

Being high on the relationship orientation and also high on the task orientation is called the 'Integrated' type, while high relationship orientation with low task orientation is the 'Related' type. Low relationship orientation with high task orientation is the 'Dedicated' type, and low relationship orientation with low task orientation is the 'Separated' type. By measuring the effectiveness of the each of the styles, Reddin worked out the eight styles in terms of being functional and dysfunctional.

These could also be looked at in terms of the Hershey and Blanchard Situational Leadership Model as well. The 'Telling/Directing' style in the Situational Leadership Model maps along the 'Dedicated' type here and has the functional style of 'Benign Autocrat' style and the dysfunctional style of 'Autocrat'. The 'Selling' style of Situational Leadership model coincides with 'Integrated' type and includes the functional 'Executive' style and the dysfunctional style of 'Compromiser'. The 'Participating/Facilitating' style in the Situational Leadership Model corresponds to 'Related' type here having the functional style of 'Developer' and the dysfunctional style of 'Missionary'. And the 'Delegating' style of the situational Leadership model maps with the 'Separated' type here covering the functional style of 'Bureaucrat' and the dysfunctional style of 'Deserter'.

The 'Deserter' style is characterized by being extremely detached from the leadership process itself with a laissez–faire approach. His not wanting to take responsibility, assume charge or create an ambience for change also makes him appear to have logged out of the managerial process itself at times. The 'Bureaucrat' style has a high dependence on creating standards, rules and standard operating procedures for most work and processes. They tend to be systematic with clear statement of policies and authority.

The 'Missionary' style has the distinct identity of being excessively accenting congeniality and amity in the workplace with avoidance of conflicts and reluctance to face or take hard choices and decisions. The 'Developer' style on the other hand has a concern for people, but tempers it with the need to complete tasks and meet organizational commitments. The accent is towards the growth and development of the people with participation in the knowledge sharing and competency development.

The 'Compromiser' style has the difficulty of integrating a concern for people with the concern for tasks in the organizational processes often vacillating between them and largely finding himself under pressure from both sides. The 'Executive' style has the outlook of getting the team to get involved in the processes within the organization and getting a buy-in from them. They tend to be consultative and prefer the team participate in the decision processes as well.

The 'Autocrat' style is the tough taskmaster one. He tends to accent the completion of tasks to an inordinately high degree to the exclusion of any concern for the people element in the process. They are often critical and intolerant of errors, cold and distant from the people he has to manage. The 'Benign Autocrat' style on the other hand is the communicative and supportive side of being high on task orientation. They tend to be clear in their instructions and are supportive in completions of tasks assigned, while being strict and adhering to not tolerating errors.

The Reddin model is an excellent tool to understand the leadership styles and also get an inventory of the inclinations of the coachee. When used with the questionnaire to help map the style preferences of the coachee, the clarity of understanding of the leadership processes and the different dimensions of it come through easily. This is often the tool of choice for beginning the exploration and discussion on leadership. Customizing and interpreting the approaches for the coachee appear best done by the coach at a later time.

THE SITUATIONAL LEADERSHIP MODEL

Professor Paul Hershey and Ken Blanchard developed the Situational Leadership theory and model propounding the idea that there is no one style that is the best in leadership. Leadership is effective depending on its task relevance of the style and the ability to adapt to what they called the maturity level of the people being led or influenced.

The Hershey-Blanchard Situational Leadership Theory is built on two fundamental concepts—the leadership style and the maturity of the individual or group. Hershey-Blanchard looked at the leadership style in terms of the extent of task-focused behaviour and the people-focused behaviour expressed. They categorized the behaviours into four styles:

S1:   Telling—The leader provides all the direction and instructions and is involved in a one-way communication with the people—individual or group.

S2:   Selling—Here, while the leader still provides the direction, he provides a two-way communication opportunity and consults with the people, working out a buy-in into the work process.

S3:   Participating—The decision-making is shared and the leader prefers to take a less task-focused and more people- and relationship-focused approach.

S4:   Delegating—While the leader is still involved in the decision process, he prefers to let the responsibility and process be passed over to the people, and the leader takes on the monitoring role.

There may not be one preferred style construed to be the best. Hershey-Blanchard emphasize the need for the leader to be flexible and capable of donning the role that would be appropriate under the circumstance and situation he finds himself in.

The correctness and success of the style adopted is also influenced by the nature of the people being led. Hershey and Blanchard have worked out a four-level categorization to calibrate the maturity level of the people. Knowing the maturity level of the people being led helps the leader understand how they respond under different situations and circumstances.

M1: The skill level is low or specific skill is found wanting, the willingness to take up the task or the responsibility for it is also low.

M2: While the ability to take up the task or the responsibility is low, they are willing to take up the task.

M3: The ability and experience to take up the task is high, but they do not exhibit the confidence and willingness to take up the task.

M4: The ability and experience match the requirements of the task and their willingness to take responsibility and the confidence levels are also high.

The nature of the tasks involved also dictates the maturity levels of the people. While the willingness, confidence and motivation may be high in some cases, the skill and ability to perform to the levels expected may be falling short. In this kind of cases, the leader needs to take the call. It also devolves on to the leader, the ability to motivate the people and nurture dedication and commitment in them.

THE ALLPORT, VERNON AND LINDSEY STUDY OF VALUES

In 1931, Gordon W. Allport, Phillip E. Vernon and Gardner E. Lindsey put forth a study of human values categorizing values into six major types. Several studies and researches into the field have extended its validity and also carried it to further intricacies. The Allport, Vernon and Lindsey model has been a good guide for the understanding of values as espoused by people and the effects it has on their perspectives and behaviours.

The categories they had worked out were: (a) *Theoretical*: the concern or pursuit of truth through reasoning and systematic thinking; (b) *Economic*: interest in usefulness and practicability; (c) *Aesthetic*: interest in beauty, form and artistic harmony; (d) *Social*: concern for human relations and people; (e) *Political*: interest in power and influencing other people; and (f) *Religion*: in spirituality and unity, and understanding the cosmos as a whole.

Although fallen into disuse due to the current feeling that the aspects included here do not cover all facets of values in currency in the modern thinking, and coupled with the use of archaic language and references, the study still stands as one of the most respected and useful studies in the field.

The extended questionnaire asks the respondents to pick, weigh and prioritize sets of values seen under different circumstances. This results in an indication of the strength and accent given by the respondent to the particular value. The questionnaire may suffer from the respondent not being able to relate to the circumstances appearing in some parts. The questionnaire has been updated and a copyrighted version of it had appeared in 2003 in Elsevier Science.

THE 360-DEGREE FEEDBACK

The 360-degree Feedback as a tool comes in very handy in the Executive Coaching process. Many organizations today have institutionalized the process of the 360-degree Feedback. They have found it very useful and of help to the managers in being in touch with how they and their actions are perceived and received by the people around them. This also serves as an indication of the impact of performance.

The 360-degree Feedback is often programmed to be an online exercise with a constituency of people around the manager—a sample of the direct reportees, peers, the direct supervisor, seniors in the organizational set-up, internal and external clients and customers— providing the feedback. This is often a controlled and structured exercise. Most questions in the questionnaire are direct and close-ended with a few left open to evoke unstructured responses. Most organizations prefer the manager himself choosing the respondents from each category within the constituency, although a few organizations do let the manager's boss make the choice.

Caselet 7 **Who Owns Feedback?**

Harishankar Prasad Pandey, Director (HR), was clear in his mind. "We have this elaborate mechanism in place, investing so much of resources—money, time, effort and people—to set up and run the scheme. Now why should it not serve the organization's purpose first and then look at how it can be put to use to help individuals? We certainly will be taking into consideration the data that will be generated from the 360-degree Feedback at least for the senior management cadres in deciding their readiness for promotion or other forms of reward."

This was his refrain at any forum he would address in the organization.

The organization is huge and spread across several global location and is one of the leaders in the sector in India. It has grown from a small family-run organization to a genuine Indian multinational with highly trained professionals running the company now. The L&D team of the Corporate HR had worked assiduously and hard over the past few years to make the Feedback mechanism work well. The 360-degree Feedback as a developmental tool was designed and introduced during the tenure of the previous Director. Dr Bhabhani Dasgupta had envisioned it as a support to the continuing self-development efforts for the senior team in understanding the impact they have on their teams and their peers in the organization. He had championed it during its introduction and customising the design of it in the organization.

The 360-degree Feedback was designed to be voluntary and self-directed. As an indicator to help understand self and look to planning development and improvements in the team, the instrument had a slow start in the first year. But it has gained tremendous popularity over the next couple of years and is now an intervention of choice for almost all in the senior team and most in the levels below.

And then, Dr Dasgupta moved to head some other function in the organization and Harishankar Pandey stepped in. Being the practical man he had the reputation of being, he took it on himself to the leverage the popularity of the instrument to the advantage of the organizational activity. From being a voluntary instrument, it was made mandatory. The supervising manager was given access to the analyzed data along with the comments of the consultant who had been handholding the interpretation process over the couple of years. This was two years ago.

"During the first year, I had asked for feedback from my juniors and peers who were critical and could give me some hard feedback. This year, I have stayed with the safe ones because, I know I am being considered for some sensitive assignments next cycle," confides a senior executive in the bulk manufacturing plant.

Another head of a critical department says that he would rather have his people give a true picture of what they think than have some additional exercise to duplicate the annual appraisal exercise.

The consultant finds the data over the past couple of years highlighting much more of positive feedback only. The developmental content in the feedback mechanism is increasingly difficult to discern. The HR department sits in an unenviable position of having to administer the process as directed by the top, while working to guard the goodwill the intervention has garnered over the years.

The feedback is usually delivered or recorded anonymously with the respondents ticking off against boxes indicating their perspective in each question, and may also have some left open for any open-ended or descriptive comments. The questionnaire may be detailed covering areas of performance, leadership, attitude, team work, organization orientation, etc.

The 360-degree Feedback is usually intended to an indicator for the managers to reflect upon the unseen and unrecognized traits and aspects of themselves that surface during the course of their managerial functioning. The feedback mechanism works well when administered and coordinated well. The organizational sponsorship of the instrument and the process also tends to lend credibility to it.

For the process to acquire high credibility and be put to effective use, it must be treated as what it is meant to be—a feedback. Feedback is indicative and suggestive for action. It cannot ideally be taken as an evaluation of the performance of individuals while serving as feedback. Some organizations have chosen, to varying degrees, link it to evaluation process within the organization. Ranging in use in these organizations—from being an extension of the appraisal process, to it being a factor in the reward mechanism in the organization—the 360-degree Feedback has been waylaid in function beyond what its name suggests.

As an employee development instrument, its input into and utility in the Executive Coaching process is enormous. But any form of subversion leads to decrease in its value and lesser credibility. The instrument should ideally be kept out of the purview of the evaluation function in the organization. The evaluation and reward mechanism should cultivate instruments and tools of its own. Having an evaluation and subsequently reward mechanism tagged on to the feedback instrument skews the intent of both the subject and the respondent. The subject manager may attempt to pack the list with pliable respondents to get a favourable review, and the respondents may attempt to settle scores with the subject using this as opportunity.

Anonymity is also crucial in the 360-degree Feedback process. People tend to be honest in their expression of opinion when they have an assurance of confidentiality. In some instances, however, their identities could be guessed or figured out. This could turn out to be the bane of the process. The organizational climate, where there is a significant degree of conflict and mistrust, may also act to subvert the proper use of the 360-degree Feedback.

Further on, critical to the process is the use of the data generated in the process. Great care must be taken in handling the results emanating from the use of the instrument. Access to the data is a sensitive issue and must be handled with extreme care as the credibility of the process could be at stake here. Bosses, having access to and going through the data, may form judgemental opinions about their subordinates based on it. This definitely is not a desirable thing.

Just as important is the manner in which the data is presented to the subject. People tend to hear criticism louder and register them faster than praise, and react accordingly. The recipients should ideally be coached to receive feedback and be helped to interpret feedback in the right perspective.

Most organizations prefer to have an expert help people interpret, understand and plan their actions from the 360-degree Feedback. The expert helps the individual understand the significance of the numbers, clusters and statistical computations derived from the questionnaire analysis. This leads to a discussion on the variance between the individual's own perception of his actions and the impact on others, and that of others around him.

The expert, and in some cases the executive coach where present, works with the individual to chart a course of action or change that can help the individual become more effective. Where the feedback instrument is put to evaluative use, the supervisor concerned or the boss of the individual either conducts the discussion or is involved with the expert in the discussion.

When a culture and milieu conducive to coaching exists in the organization, the 360-degree Feedback process will work well and help in not only generating good, credible and useful developmental data and indicators, but also help the managers plan and execute positive change. Executive Coaching could plug in to the use of this instrument to derive enormous advantages in helping the coachees see themselves for who they are and how they are experienced by others. This augurs well for use in a pre- and post-intervention indicator of progress and change for the coachee in the Executive Coaching process.

OTHER MODELS AND TOOLS

There abound other tools and instruments to help calibrate different aspects of the coachee in terms of personality, attitude, capability, skills, etc. The executive coach has to take a discretionary

call on whether he may want to use any or rely on his own reading as preferred by some. There are executive coaches following
certain approaches in coaching that makes the understanding of
the coachee a subjective experience. This puts the responsibility
squarely on the executive coach and the extent of his experience
and wisdom guides the accuracy of his reading. It would do the
coachee well to be aware of this and willingly accept the approach
that the executive coach has taken.

7. ISSUES FACING EXECUTIVE COACHING

EXECUTIVE COACHING IS a beneficial association between two people high on the measure of success. They are, in their own space, good at their trade and the executive coach helps the coachee excel beyond the level he is operating at, at that time. Being so, there are issues and concerns that crop up in the practice, which could veer the process off track and disrupt and destroy an otherwise great thing going. These issues can be contentious and niggling; sometimes tangible and manifest; and at other times, subliminal and veiled. They can be vicious and virulent at times, and lie dormant for long periods and strike at unguarded moments.

It is good to be aware of their existence even if they don't afflict the practitioner or the beneficiary at the present time. Precaution and inoculation against their occurrence is a good guarantee against tripping over them unwittingly. Some of the significant ones are discussed here, but it would be prudent to also be vigilant against the lesser ones unlisted and in hibernation within.

VICARIOUS ANIMATION OF LIFE SCRIPT

Executive coaches are human too but the calling of being a coach often requires them to leave behind what would be normal failings for other folks. They cannot give in when they are the scaffolds that prop other people up. That is often the biggest burden that gets yoked on to them by the very nature of their chosen profession.

Even so, a few shortcomings do crawl in under the door and they can become significant irritants. At times, they may manifest as major liabilities, even derailing the process. One such infestation is the transference of the life script of the executive coach on to the coachee. In moments of weakness, a few coaches do tend to animate their own unfulfilled life script and live them through the life of their coachees.

Life script is a plan one hopes life could be lived by. This is often followed by individuals in trying to fulfil their wishes and desires. While those parts that do get achieved leave a feeling of satisfaction, unfulfilled parts do leave behind a residual craving and a fond hope for fructification sometime in future. So long as the striving for successful closure and the feeling of having lived their life script is confined to the individual himself, it is legitimate and acceptable. However, a few amongst us do intrude into someone else's life trying to impose or get them to co-opt their life script—through persuasion or coercion—to vicariously experience their own life script through others.

Against this subliminal tendency of vicariously living their unfulfilled script, the executive coach should be ever vigilant. They do not walk in in broad daylight or in overt action, but some form of it does leak in and perhaps stains the corners of what would otherwise be a clean practice. It is not that this does happen to all, but unrecognized infestations need to be handled with care and meticulous concern.

UNCLEAR AGENDA

Executive Coaching is a sequential process with a targeted outcome. This requires the coach, and therefore the coachee, to be adequately clear as to what they are working towards and where they are headed. The ideal would be to chart the course of action at the outset so as to have a route map to navigate through the process.

However, not all processes progress along prescribed paths. Deviations, distractions and even derailments are not uncommon. These may result from any number of reasons, throwing the progression in plans out of gear. While experienced executive coaches can see these coming and may recognize the symptoms before the malady manifests itself, a few may be caught unaware.

All too often, it is the change in business environment, unforeseen realignment of organizational structure and placements, changes in the coachee's personal life, shift in priorities of the coachee, unforeseen shift in relationship between the coachee and the executive coach, burden of extraneous factors increasing, shifting and unclear goals or even changes in executive coach's life. It is any or all of these that could be the reason for the halt or slowing down of the progress in the process.

Caselet 8 This One's for You

K.S.V.V. Prasad sat slumped in the chair. He was one of the high-fliers in the company and everyone had really high expectations from him. He was the youngest Director in the company history. He had the image of a go-getting achiever.

This was the eighth session he was having in the Executive Coaching series. He laced his fingers and supported his chin with his knuckles. His head bobbed up and down as he spoke slowly. "I don't know what to do with myself over the next 10 years. I really don't have any targets or objectives I want to set for myself."

This was a different song today. Prasad has had a different objective he has set for himself each time he came into the session. It appeared that the goal depended on who his current advisor was. After the first session, he said he would seriously give his life goals a thought before setting up the work in the next session. And sure enough, he had talked extensively in the following session about working towards taking to entrepreneurship after putting in five years. He had even prepared what he called a blueprint for his entrepreneurial plans in meticulously detail—from the timeframes to the financing and revenue details, the technology sourcing and staffing, etc. It was very impressive and surely serious for someone who has invested so much to work out the details.

Two week later, the entrepreneurship plans were given a quick burial. That session revolved around how he could easily be the regional director in five years, at least for the Asia–Pacific region in the company itself. The following week, Prasad migrated to working on new emerging technology platform. A month later, he thought he would like to take a sabbatical from work to pursue his passion to compose for the rock band he played with on weekends.

There was so much he would invest in working out each plan in fine detail and be so focused and serious about each one. And then today, finally he was confessing to confusion. "There is so much I want out of life that I don't know what I want," he said. "I know I am capable of getting to what I set my mind on. I always have, but I seem to be doing and achieving all this because someone else has set me to it. My parents, my teacher, my sister, my best friends, my wife... and now... I know I want to impress you, but I can't figure out what you want me to do."

The direct result of this—or in a sense the casualty—is the agenda drawn up in the initial stages of the process. While a certain level of flexibility would be built into the agenda set out, it does not accommodate wide fluctuations and drastic unplanned overhauling. Clarity of agenda is a requisite for smooth and fruitful progress in the Executive Coaching process. Unclear or ambiguous agenda retards any form of positive movement forward.

The difficulty in this is that the problem does not announce itself until the infestation has taken hold and recovery becomes arduous. Therefore, guarding against losing track of or heading into fuzziness in agenda is definitely good. Often, experience and wisdom of the executive coach may pre-empt and help recover at the right time, but being on guard helps. All the same, the caution is not to sacrifice flexibility in the process while trying not to lose track of the agenda or target.

BIAS-LED APPROACH

Bias is some form of mental dust mite that thrives in the invisible crevices of our mind. As the crevices gather dust and waste due to poor mental housekeeping, biases thrive and flourish. They don't crawl out to announce themselves but eventually take over our mental processes and regulate our thinking along their own subverted programmed lines.

Executive coaches who often question and seek to dust off their thinking do keep the freshness and openness in good and healthy condition. Free from possible bias, they are able to work with their coachee in ways that are best for them. Clearing out possible bias in any interaction or issue should be the constant endeavour.

The key to minimizing and eventually eliminating bias is heightened self-awareness. Knowing oneself in all aspects tends to keep the executive coach in touch with the personal, social and often the intimate processes of the mind. Aware of how these processes work out and proceed, the coach can be on watch for any possible bias that may creep in.

Also, being in constant interaction with the outside environment and people sharpens the ability to realize possible positions of bias that may unconsciously work their way in. The awareness also helps in taking a position of objectivity and stay above the matter and issue at hand.

EMOTIONAL DEPENDENCY TRAP

Executive Coaching is a close-proximity and emotionally-wired experience. And being so, can lead to attachments and relationship detours not wholly planned. The extent of intimacy shared, and the help-giver and help-receiver nature of the process opens the association out to the possibility. Emotional dependency can take the form of decision dependence, infatuation, emotional or sensual entanglements.

Emotional dependency can be emotional attachment or addiction of one to the other or circumstances that can lend comfort through contact. The risk is particularly high with emotionally vulnerable individuals, cross gender associations and young coachees unable to contend with authority figures. All transgressions on this plane are clear violations of accepted ethics in Executive Coaching.

The primary responsibility for restraint and caution devolves on to the executive coach. He must guard against deviations from the path of the accepted relationship and the extent of association in Executive Coaching. Ideally, he must be aware of the tenor of relationship at all times and head off any possible deviations. Emotional dependence is hard to resolve and does negate achievements in other aspects of the coaching process.

TRANSFERENCE OF AMBITIONS

Ambitions are constant companions and a necessary part of the success of high achievers. It is what drives them to outdo themselves and crave for that restless striving to edge over the next summit—each time and every time. But then, there comes a time when one realizes that there may still be ambitions as yet unrealized and is well past the time when one may still have a shot at the accomplishment. It is there that some do not see the reality for what it is and look to vicarious forms of fulfilment.

Normally the executive coach should have worked past the risk of having festering unrealized ambitions. These issues should ideally have been sorted out earlier and the present reality accepted. However, the failing of lesser people does pursue a few amongst the august class of executive coaches. It is these few that need to be alert of harming their coachees, even if unwittingly.

The unrealized ambitions have a knack of creeping up from behind and hitching a ride on any proxy who is weak enough not to see them for what they are. The coach too at times does not realize that he is actually fostering their own agenda and aspiration on to the coachee to achieve. This gives some sort of a vicarious pleasure of triumph and success. However small these may eventually turn out to be, it is playing hopscotch with ethics.

The agenda, the plans and strategies for the coachee should, in its entirety, be formulated keeping the coachee in mind and in his best interests. The slightest temptation to let the executive coach's own ambitions and agenda hitch a ride on the energy, verve or achievements of the coachee should be put down in the first instance itself. This is so much an expression of personal ethical stand as it has to be regulated at the individual level.

POSSESSIVENESS

The Executive Coaching brings the coach and the coachee in the range of reciprocally intimate setting. The very nature of the close association and working makes for the closeness and the strong bond of relationship. But then the context and the protocol set for the relationship should ideally be clear in defining the boundaries and terms of engagement. That the association and the context of the relationship are not of a permanent nature should be well-grasped by both.

Sometimes, however, there exists the risk of emotions engaging beyond the bounds of control; misread cues and signals; motives, not wholly legitimate or warranted, stepping in; or even the simple fact of not knowing when to disengage; may result in attachments that work to the detriment of the process and participants in Executive Coaching. It is in these cases that excessive possessiveness creeps in and the benefits of the engagement get compromised.

There will come a time in the Executive Coaching process where the relationship context will have to be changed and the coaching relationship will have to work its way to an end. Not that the relationship between the coach and the coachee has to terminate, but the engagement will no longer be the same. Even so, the coachee will have to move on and at times engage some other coach in the context of the current needs. The coach, for his part, should not get so attached to his coachee that he would find it difficult or deter in his steps towards disengagement. The executive coach too will have to move on, beyond the present, to other assignments that may come his way. Either of them should not limit his ability to disengage the association and move on.

ACCEPTING LIMITATIONS

There would certainly be a few among us who are well-versed in most issues and areas of knowledge. But the rest of us must accept that there are areas that are beyond our reach. This is the hard part.

The executive coach is often subject to searching enquiry regarding a host of things. They can range from the most mundane and innocuous to the most philosophical, profound and intellectual. This, he must be able to navigate through well enough to keep his credibility high and build a reputation for being good at his craft. The coachee has, and rightfully so, high faith in the knowledge and capability of the coach he is associated with. It is up to the coach to live up to this.

At the same time, there will always be areas that the coach may not be adequately equipped to handle or work in. These are not let-downs but an acceptable fact of the makeup of everyone. The executive coach may not have adequate expertise in certain areas and it would be best for the coachee to refer to or engage in work with someone else. The executive coach must ideally have the humility to acknowledge this and also be open enough to discuss the matter with the coachee. The areas of limitation often are in the areas of medical realm of mental health, emotional health or physical health. The executive coach may not have sufficient expertise to work with issues in these areas. He must ideally acknowledge his limitations and refer the coachee to professionals better placed to deal with the matter.

The maturity and the confidence of the executive coach in himself will stand by him in taking the call in such matters. Executive coaches who are secure about their own standing and are not out to seek approval in each of their actions and work would be best placed to acknowledge this. The cause of doing what is best for the coachee would be well-served in accepting the limitations of one's own specialization and the areas of expertise.

NEED TO APPLY REFERRAL SKILLS

Executive Coaching has at its heart the interest and the development of the coachee. Therefore, the executive coach should ideally keep in mind that when it comes to giving the coachee the best, even the coach himself should not be a hurdle. The best available in the field and accessible should be provided for the coachee to utilize.

The executive coach should be on guard against feeling uncomfortable in referring the coachee to other sources of expertise, preferring to work with or deal with the issues on his own. Then again, there comes a time when the executive coach could be called upon to recommend that the coachee consult some other professional better placed to deal with the issue at hand. He will have to diagnose the underlying bases for the issue not being resolved between them and then work out what kind of expertise is needed. The executive coach will also have to look for someone who would fit the requirement. Very often, matters of this nature come up when there are issues of mental health, emotional health or even medical issues involved. There are professionals in the specific fields who would certainly be better placed to work with these issues.

The problematic issue will be when the coach is reluctant to exercise the need to refer the coachee to others for whatever reason. The reasons may be: various insecurities in the executive coach; his inability to diagnose what the difficulty is; referral abilities in the coach may be low; or the coach may be unwilling to share the time of working with the coachee with another professional.

These work to the detriment of the coachee in the end, even though he may not know of the issue being present or may be too enamoured by the perceived abilities of the executive coach that he does not see the flaw. The association and the dynamics between the executive coach and the coachee being confidential and normally not subject to review, the chances of this coming to light is pretty low. However, the coachee is within his right to request for another opinion in case he disagrees with the coach on any issue or strategy. The success of this approach depends on how the issue is handled.

TRAPPED IN TRANSACTIONAL ISSUES

As in the classical example, Executive Coaching is not about providing fish, but about teaching how to fish. The entire focus of the effort is on how the coachee can transform himself into a better and more successful person over the longer term. The work entails much more of visualizing the possible goals to be achieved and the targets to shoot for. In that sense, the Executive Coaching is intended to achieve long-term excellence.

Executive Coaching cannot be shackled by short-term or myopic issues or concerns. These do tend to become the undergrowth that obscure the path and, in some cases, lead the entire process astray. During the course of association with the executive coach, it is tempting to use his counsel to work through immediate problems being faced or to sort out difficulties that are burdensome at the present moment. These issues and concerns do not have any long-term significance and may not even be remembered in some time. They are the weeds that clog the natural flow in the Executive Coaching process.

These issues are normally transactional in nature and can be seen as an anxiety on how a specific subordinate or colleague who has a particular contention has to be handled; how to tell the boss about not being able to report a particular data on time; when the best time would be to call a meeting on a particular contentious issue in the workplace, etc. These are decisions to be taken and issues to be resolved by the coachee on his own rather than seek the involvement of the executive coach in the matter.

When the coachee is sufficiently senior in the organization, mature enough and experienced enough, they tend to keep the interactions with the executive coach within the realms of the coaching context itself. But among the younger or less experienced executives, the temptation to pick the brains of the executive coach simply because he is available is high. This tendency needs to be guarded against. These transactional issues increase the dependence of the coachee on the executive coach to provide solutions to immediate issues and also lose sight of the long-term objectives of the intervention.

Ideally, the executive coach should be alert to the coachee slipping into this and head-off any possibility of this tendency becoming a habit. An occasional help in checking the perspective of the executive coach on as immediate problem faced by the coachee helps to understand how the coachee may be using the learning from the intervention. But repeated occurrences should set-off sirens.

STATURE TRAP

Every organization has hierarchy of some form. And for people within, their position in these hierarchies are the expression of their worth to the system and the organization itself. In most cases, it is also a relative measure of the importance between people working within the organization.

These hierarchies are sometimes traps that ensnare even level-headed people into believing that they are statements about the people themselves. These positions also translate themselves into protocols that bind and restrict people in their interactions and relationships. When such infirm equations also get soaked with insecurities that people carry, it becomes a heady and explosive mixture.

People's insecurities, often arising out their capabilities not matching their desires for recognition and rewards, lead them to lean on their acquired positions to gain stature in the system. These excessive emphases on the acquired stature prevent them from being open to honest inventory of their capabilities and developing themselves further. It builds a false sense of protective sanctuary around the individual and thwarts any form of functional and productive association in coaching.

Executive Coaching, or for that matter any learning, is best carried out in an environment shorn of external status or stature. When this cannot be achieved in full measure, the effort is that much devalued resulting in less than adequate returns. The executive coach should recognize the games that organizations and those within indulge in and steer clear of them for the good health of the coaching process. The coachee, for his part, has to recognize the impediment in the trap and rise above it.

MANAGERIAL ENVIRONMENT VERSUS COACHING ENVIRONMENT

Executive Coaching functions in a learning environment. This entails both the executive coach and the coachee being open and not stuck in any prior or external hierarchical context in the interaction and relationship. There is a sense of egalitarian equity implied here. However, the 'normal' world they come from or return to after each coaching session, does not espouse this equity. This calls for a shift each time they enter the environment or exit it.

Recognizing it may be easy, but not letting one leak into the other is difficult. The behaviours, feelings and also attitudes that seep in with the leakage do contaminate the setting to some extent. This does reduce or delay the effectiveness of the efforts invested.

Then again, it is important that the coach takes cognizance of the fact that he operates in a different environment than the coachee in the 'real' life outside the coaching environment. The coachee is being prepared to make himself more effective and grow in the outside environment and not so much in the partly sanitized environment of Executive Coaching. This must be constantly kept in mind and all activities and discussions should take this into consideration. It does sometimes happen that the 'reality' may get missed.

The whole issue of the managerial environment vs the coaching environment should be evaluated ahead of any design being contemplated or put in place. And then again, any element of conflict between the two must be worked out ahead of any experimental activity being tried out. The executive coach carries the burden of responsibility in monitoring this at all times.

8. BUILDING COACHING CULTURE IN ORGANIZATIONS

THE ORGANIZATIONAL CULTURE almost always dictates what practices will germinate, grow and endure in the organization. The organizational culture is built on the shared expectations, practices, experiences and norms within the organization. It reflects the values, beliefs and attitudes of the people. The culture also conditions the people to feel and behave in a particular manner in conformity with it. This contributes to their comfort and sense of being accepted within the organizational community.

The organizational culture contributes to the ease or otherwise with which any intervention affecting people can be introduced. For the intervention to take root, get accepted and grow, it has to first be in conformity with the culture. Organizational culture can be built and steered towards positive contribution to allow introduction of any intervention that can eventually reinforce constructive aspects of the culture.

In introducing Executive Coaching as a positive L&D effort for people in an organization, either having an organizational culture that fosters such effort or building one over time to help in its acceptance is essential in the long run. There are key aspects of the organizational culture that promote Executive Coaching. They are discussed here to work out possible strategies in building such an organizational culture and ambience.

SENIOR MANAGEMENT BUY-IN

For any culture in the organization to endure, the buy-in of the senior management is essential. It is almost impossible for any form or concerted attitude, behaviour or even outlook to take root and flourish unless supported by the people at the higher branches of the hierarchy. Expected and preferred behaviours are encouraged and therefore allowed to be practiced. Other sequences of conduct are discouraged or put down. This eventually crystallizes as the organizational culture identity.

It is therefore imperative that the senior management must want to establish a coaching culture within the organization for it to take root and grow. Ideally, not only should the senior management be supportive of the need to establish the culture, but also be willing to practice and be seen to be practicing it. The support encourages the practitioners and the support functionaries as well.

Any of the members of the senior management being a coach himself; or being available for sessions in coaching; or at some time, having been a coach earlier; or being available to coaches within the organization to shared perspectives; could go a long way in creating the right image for coaching as a process. There may also be instances of any of the members of the senior management being recipient of Executive Coaching himself.

Supportive behaviour and orientation, in wanting to be a part of organizational coaching activities, encouraging coaches to participate and be part of the coaching initiatives, being willing to provide supportive logistical and other supports, being receptive to the coaching-related initiatives by HR and line functionaries, valuing learning and development activities, etc., add depth and value to the worth being placed on the creation of coaching culture within the organization. Whosoever the process owner down the line in the coaching initiative, the senior management's interest and buy-in are essential components in the fostering of a coaching-friendly culture.

LONGEVITY OF CORPORATE IDENTITY

For favourable coaching culture to take root and get established in the organization, it is often necessary for the people to feel that the corporate image and identity are fairly stable and favourable. The identity that the company has in the outside world with which the people can associate and relate to has to also have a degree of permanence.

The need for the people to feel proud to be associated with the organization will help in making them think that investing in the company's culture is worth the effort. Since most people feel that investing in people below them, down in the hierarchy, is an investment for the organization, they need to get the sense that the effort is good and credible.

Towards this end, it is the responsibility of the senior management to ensure that the corporate identity and image is immaculate and is held in high regard by the world outside. This contributes to the image being high within itself. This can be achieved through visible and espoused practices such as ethical and moral conduct in business, respect for the environment and community, respect for the individual, etc. Not only does the beliefs and practices have to be seen but also spoken about and propagated for the building up of good corporate image. Thus, this will help in building a positive and enduring organizational culture within.

EXCELLENCE AND QUALITY ORIENTATION

Wanting to be the best, and not just among the best, is a powerful propellant. Further, a firm commitment to quality in all aspects of organizational life is a strong driving force towards not tolerating anything less. This is an exceptionally strong foundation to have in building a coaching culture. Having this as a value firmly embedded in the organizational psyche would move the people to seek ways to achieve it in some form. Coaching as an accepted form of growth and building up of competency all around will be realized, in most parts, as the best way to achieve this.

The natural corollary is the growth and establishment of a coaching-friendly culture itself in the organization, with the beliefs, practices and attitudes that support the introduction and growth of the intervention.

Wanting this to happen is one thing, and getting people to believe and practise it as a norm, is quite another. The excellence and quality orientation can be framed in the organization through a systematic campaign beginning with awareness, creating widespread acceptance, active implementation and moving slowly but surely towards zero-tolerance towards anything less than the highest level of excellence and quality. The route is fraught with several challenges and temptations to compromise and scale-down, accept and carry on and, in a sense, 'be like everyone else'. But then if there is a determination and buy-in from the top, the path becomes that much easier.

Ideally, this campaign as a part of the culture-building effort should start with a value statement from the top and the strategy for implementation of it through the organization. The process owner and the champions could be identified to make the effort concerted and focused.

The closer the organization is to making excellence and quality orientation a reality, the easier it will be for the establishment and fostering of coaching-friendly culture within. Then again, this culture and the orientation are mutually supportive of quality and excellence-focus, and work towards strengthening and ensuring good health in both.

COMPETITION IS PERFORMANCE-DRIVEN AND NOT PERSONAL

Coaching, and particularly Executive Coaching, is driven by the desire to be the best and therefore thrives in the spirit of competition. A competitive environment invigorates the participants in the system and also infuses energy into it. An organization driven by competition would strive to succeed and settle for no less.

However, competition also brings with it some seamy sides that should be well guarded against and prevented from infecting other aspects of the culture within. Competition can bring out some intense expressions of aggression in various forms that may be detrimental to harmony and goodwill that otherwise would exist. Connivance and manipulation follows and over time may lead to the vitiation of the culture and amity within.

Then again, competition need not be vicious and can be converted to being healthy and even universally helpful. Towards this, it is essential that the rules of engagement in competition, especially internal, are clearly drawn. The top-to-down cascade of the value of internal constructive competition being positive and not mutually detrimental has to be taken very seriously. All forms and expressions of viciousness, resentment and disrespect to this core belief should be forcefully put down. Then and only then can the power of positive internal competition be harnessed for the good of the people and the organization.

This needs a strong endorsement and visible practice from the senior management and cascaded down the hierarchy for the culture to take firm root. There is also caution to be exercised in trying to establish this element of culture—being a double-edged weapon, it could cut either ways. The initiative to create excellence without conflict is a tremendous culture-building move towards promoting coaching efforts in the organization.

NURTURING AND GROWTH-ORIENTED

The substantive part of the organizational culture should give the feeling to people that the organization is supporting its people. The orientation of the policies, processes and norms are towards the good of not only the organization but also the growth and development of the people. The overarching concern is for respect and concern for the individual while in the pursuit of the primary organizational objectives. While the character of the organization is certainly commercial or with a decided profit-motive, it is not pursued at the cost of the well-being of the people who make the profits happen. The organization and its people are engaged in a symbiotic relationship to maximize mutual gains.

This does not fly in the face of the authority and established hierarchy in the organization, nor is it a votary for democratization of the system. It seeks to place people in the scheme of things in the organization without compromising the basic character. The equation of the organization making adequate investment in the development and provision of opportunity for its people, and the people, in turn, offering higher productivity is the balance that makes for good organizational culture. This being demonstrated across the organization would help build a nurturing and growth-oriented culture.

The overarching concern is for the individuals improving themselves while in pursuit of the primary organizational objectives. Such approach promotes positive organizational culture that nurtures and supports growth and development. As the policies so also the practices provide opportunities for people at all levels to seek learning and improvement of their competencies, skills and performance. The leaders and superiors, as a value, believe and practise helping individuals grow. The environment is non-discriminatory and fosters equity among people.

People as a result tend to be positive and inclined to utilize all avenues of development. Such environment builds and sustains a nurturing and growth-oriented culture. Coaching as a development initiative takes root easily in such environments.

Such a culture is the ideal. Anywhere close enough to the ideal is good as this would provide the best substratum for the introduction of positive L&D interventions like Executive Coaching with ease. These would also gain high level of acceptance and therefore move ahead in reinforcing the virtues of such organizational culture.

It is definitely easy in description and difficult in implementation. But it is well within the realm of the possible as there are several organizations that have successfully worked their way close to the ideal. Such affirmative organizational culture also requires a level of stability and maturity of the organization. Older organizations often have a head start in being able to craft such cultures.

TRANSPARENT SINCERITY AND AUTHENTICITY

'Walk the Talk', they say, is most convincing. This cannot be truer when it comes to the ambience and milieu in the organization. Organizational culture has a large element of perception of it going into its making. How the people perceive the policies, processes and practices governs their idea of what the culture is all about.

Consequently, not only have the policies and rules in the organization got to be clear, equitable and stated, but they also have to be perceived and seen to be so. So, also the consistency of practices and working of the processes with the stated policies and rules is desirable. This consistency should be practiced by all people across the length and breadth of the hierarchy.

To carry this forward, transparency of processes and openness in relationship help build confidence of the people in the organizational climate. As far as is possible, the practices and organizational interactions, the implementation of policies and the affairs of the organization should ideally be managed in such a manner that they will stand open scrutiny. They may not necessarily be in the open, but they should ideally be carried out believing that they could be open, if need be. Such belief in transparency can create a culture devoid of internecine intricacies.

The practices and dealings at all levels of the organization should be based on the belief in the value of honesty and authenticity. They should be valued high on ethical standards. The people who are responsible for the organizational culture equity should believe in being true to their ethical commitments.

This again is a statement of the ideal and the striving should be to be at or as near the ideal as can be. The culture that grows out of such beliefs and practices provides excellent ground for people growing with high ethical standards themselves and also helping inculcating it in the others within. This works well for the L&D to have a high value in such cultures.

BELONGINGNESS AND STRONG ORGANIZATIONAL IDENTIFICATION

Identification with the organization does not come easily. It takes the better part of good effort and convincing reasons for people to invest emotionally in the organization and be willing to identify themselves closely with it. But then, when this is in place, the dividends from it are enormous.

The ideal would seem to be a little distance away all the time, but working towards it is the essence of trying to build and retain an organizational culture conducive to positive development interventions. Executive Coaching requires comfort of the people in the organization with the environment and ambience and their feeling secure within it. Coaches do not have the time or the leeway to work with the security issues in the organizational culture. This is more to do with their not being able to have the reach and also the resources within the organization to make any significant change in it as a whole. Further, it is also for their trade to gain respectability and acceptance within the organization, and for their coachees to feel their development efforts, can be put to use within and for the organization.

A good point to leverage is the fact that working towards building a strong sense of belongingness also works to reduce the level of interpersonal conflicts within the organization. This is particularly true in organizations deeply rooted in the Indian traditional values and practices where paternalism and familial affinities are strong and are valued. The strong organizational identity also works well to bind the people in the organization closer together and work to keep employee attrition low. This gives a good opportunity for long-term career and employee development planning. All these contribute much towards coaching as a culture taking root and blossoming, thus making the work of the executive coach in such an organization much easier. Also, the practice is accorded a higher stature in such cultures.

WISDOM IS ACCORDED RESPECT AND RECOGNITION

Among the most valued assets for any organization is the intangible accumulation of knowledge gained and experience accumulated over the years of its existence. All too often, these are never documented or calculated in the estimation of worth. These assets are locked in people who have invested in staying and working with the organization over the years.

Wisdom garnered over time is as valuable an asset as any that are traded or calibrated. Organizations that are able to nurture and build on these are those that leverage their people assets well. It is for this reason that the organizational culture must be sensitized to recognizing the learning and wisdom that has been stocked in people. This is not to be mistaken for the rank that 'seniority' gets in some organizations in their scheme of thing. The ability to utilize knowledge and experience tempered with discretion and the keenness to discern subtleties in issues is respected in people.

An organizational culture that values and accords respect to wisdom in the scheme of organizational life is often one that has the depth of maturity to hold the worth of years of learning and garnered knowledge in high esteem. Wisdom of any organization is the collective wisdom of its people. The wealth of the organization is not only in its physical and monetary assets, but also in the collective wisdom of its people. The realization and the consequent steps to guard the resource with respect and consideration is the mark of a mature culture.

Where wisdom is accorded respect and people who have worked towards gathering and developing it being conferred some form of recognition will encourage higher levels of learning and development initiatives within. This is the kind of ideal culture that fosters coaching and guided growth.

RECIPROCAL RESPECT FOR THE INDIVIDUAL

'Respect for the individual' has come to be accepted as a part of the core values espoused by mature organizations and is reflected in its practices across the organization. There have been even strong actions taken to enforce and send the message of the importance given to this value in the organization. Senior managers in the shop floor have been asked to quit for reasons of consistent breach of this even if they have been among the most productive in their other contributions. The value of 'respect for the individual', in a sense, defines the base culture of the organization.

The respect for the individual supports the dignity and self-esteem of the individuals working in the organization. This is, by no means, an endorsement of the tolerance of the individuals whose performance has receded below par. It is the indicator of the way people are treated in the organizational setting. The indicators of breach of the value is in the use of unacceptable language and behaviour; bullying; discrimination on basis of community, caste, geographic origin, gender or faith; and use of threat or coercion. These as an organizational policy are discouraged and put down unequivocally.

The value and belief supports and absolves errors and failures resulting from actions taken in line of work 'in good faith'. Exploration and risk-taking is encouraged and the genuineness of it is supported in the interest of the organization. Anxieties of people in the lower reaches of the hierarchy are supported to shore-up confidence and higher output at work.

The organization offers respect for the individual in return for respect for each other at all levels of the hierarchy, and also the organization. The feeling and principle encouraged is that the organization is a coming together of individuals with common interest to work towards the good of the organization. This builds and leverages the synergy generated in the process. Growth and development are as much an individual pursuit as it is an organizational goal.

Many organizations have embraced this in right earnest. Years of effort and faithful practice has gone in before it has been universally accepted within the organization. But, in the end, it has all been worth the effort as the paybacks on the investment have been the good work environment fostering excellence and drive to higher and better performance. Such environments are the ones that have cultivated effective and innovative learning and development initiatives, such as Executive Coaching.

RELATIONSHIPS ARE HEALTHY AND NOT EXPLOITATIVE

There is a level of sanctity accorded to relationships in the organization. They are bound by accepted protocols and professional norms. The relationships are networks of professional interdependence built and nurtured for mutual facilitation of professional work. Relationships, vertically and horizontally, across the hierarchy are intended for the good of the participants and the organization. They are supportive and beneficial. Each one is respected and considered as an important link in the web of organizational existence. This would be the relationship station to work towards in the organization.

An organizational culture that encourages the growth of such an approach fosters a feeling of amity and goodwill within the organization. It helps build mutual trust, and dispels suspicion and animosity. The atmosphere is ideal for working at establishing a positive and favourable culture that the organization can expand and grow at a fast pace safely in.

The relationships between people emphasize the larger good of the community and not narrow immediate gains. Traditional values and interdependence are encouraged to support expectations in the relationships and comfort levels. People seek satisfaction in association. This approach in no way implies compromise of the organizational goals and objectives in favour of the milieu within.

The culture that grows out of the absence of coercion and incursion into the space of the other, with exploitation and internecine scheming being discouraged and animosity towards others in the organizations for whatever reason being put down, helps in working towards the ideal progress and growth oriented culture.

Prime initiatives in learning and development thrive and produce excellent results in such environments.

It does take quite an amount of effort and struggle to work the culture in this direction and get to a reasonable proximity of the ideal. But it would always be worth the striving.

AMBITION TEMPERED WITH MATURITY

Ambition in individuals is the driving force that leads towards achievement and success. It is ambition that propels people to do better and be on the path to higher levels of learning and search for knowledge. Ambition often provides the extra energy to push for the stretch to attaining the extra distance or height. Ambition is a good thing—to have alive inside and to keep people awake.

In organizations, such people are valued and nurtured to provide the organization the impetus towards achieving its own goals and objectives. The mutual support and striving do work well in most cases.

However, sometimes the process could get vitiated and take a turn towards the dark side. Ambition has the bitter side to it too. It does drive people towards consideration of themselves first and ahead of the larger good that can be served in the long term. This could push people to look for short-term and narrow gains at the cost of the organizational or community well-being. People afflicted by this outlook are often those with low maturity levels and who do not have the depth to visualize the larger organizational context they are a part of.

Maturity contributed in tempering ambition to a stable and level-headed approach with an ability to channel the energy of ambition towards positive outcomes. It does help people in seeing that achievements, growth and glory can be attained without cost to someone else. That mutuality of efforts and sharing of the fruits of labour can augur better rewards.

The organization growing on the strength of people ambitions that are moderated with the mature outlook they espouse have a greater chance of long-term prosperity. Such organizational cultures provide better opportunity to seek new knowledge that supports faster attainment of ambitions. Mutual learning and interdependent growth that coaching offers can easily succeed here.

Caselet 9 The Lord Had Other Plans

A good scare, angioplasty, a stent and a new lease on life are what it took to make David Yesupadam turn over a new leaf. The first 28 years of his fast-paced marketing career in the machine tools and engineering sector were spend without looking at the speedometer of life. Adrenaline was a constant companion and the acceleration of growth was fuelled by a liberal dose of all the wrong habits. Yesupadam had raced to the top of the heap in the profession and was the reference point for the next two generations of people following him at that time. His entrepreneurial venture had succeeded beyond what Yesupadam had himself imagined he could achieve. Success, wealth and fame gushed in abundant measure. To him, enough was never enough.

And then, one late evening in the midst of celebrating a new deal with his foreign collaborators, he sank to the floor as if someone had stuck a pin into the over-inflated balloon and let the air rush out. The hotel doctor, wailing ambulance siren, emergency department, cardiac OT, ICCU and recovery in one slow-motion blurred sequence. Yesupadam was ready to lie down at the Lord's feet. "But the Lord had other plans and so He sent me back", says Yesupadam.

"To me, the heady ride of the first half of my career was necessary to get a perspective on how I should take the rest of my life. It's not me really that drove this David to what he had become. I was young then and did not think of anything beyond what would get me up the next hill. I was the fully loaded marine landing on the beachhead with the single-minded brief and determination to take the land and hold. Nothing else mattered. So, I went for it without a care for what the other consequences were.

"Looking back, in the process of logging up all the gains and taking all the companies to great profitability and wealth creation, I not only lost myself, but also destroyed so many people in the process. The environment in which I had earned my spurs did not teach me to do anything else. It just egged my unbridled ambition on. And the rush was too much to ignore and like the bull in rage I kept charging ahead. Looking back, I was a damn fool. I paid too high a price for what the environment made me do.

"Today, one and a half year after my frightening brush with tragedy, I know what I should not make the young boys and girls who work for me today do. There is a time for everything and a speed at which it must be moving ahead. I have changed so much in my organization to help these youngsters not fall into the trap I had tripped into. I must let them grow well and create a stable environment in my organization to help them understand the pace at which they must let their ambition take them forward," says Yesupadam.

In the year since Yesupadam returned to work, he has been a man possessed in overhauling the aggressive set-up he had established in his organization. He began with working on himself. He took on the services of an executive coach to walk him through the transition. Then he moved to work on his organization.

He recast his entire HR team to include people who had earlier worked with organizations that had high emphasis on L&D initiatives. He invested in people development and knowledge upgradation. His technical team was most supportive of his efforts in introducing higher emphasis on quality over target as was the old practice. The sales and marketing team was asked to stress on service over sales numbers. The organization today has a much lower attrition rate as a spin-off.

The metamorphosis was complete and Yesupadam's search for redemption has helped his organization too.

INFORMED HR SET-UP

The burden of animating the culture visualized for the organization lands at HR's door. They are eventually the ones who will have to hold the baton in the organizational race as far as any people-related system is concerned. They would be responsible for the kind of culture that evolves in the organization.

Being so, the HR has to be a mature and informed team of professionals. They should ideally have the knowledge of how culture is built, nurtured and sustained in organizations. They should have the wisdom and the sagacity to construct the kind of culture that fosters the practices supportive the organization's goals and objectives.

Therefore, HR should not only be professionally savvy in their practices but also sensitive to the environment that prevails in the organization. Their professional capabilities help build good HR systems, but a sensitive and informed HR helps build the confidence among people in the organization and the beliefs it stands for. HR should also be well-versed with the mechanics of introducing high value initiatives for the growth of the organization and development of its people. They must be in the know of things with respect to the soft technology in HR practices and framework. This is the responsibility of each member of the HR set-up for the head to the junior-most person. Each contributes significantly to making the composite image presented.

Having an informed HR, in that sense, fosters the ideal climate for initiating a coaching culture within with ease.

9. WHAT THE HR FUNCTION CAN DO

FOR THE EFFECTIVE introduction of the Executive Coaching process in the organization, it would augur well to have someone who can be called the 'process owner'. This is, in effect, the one responsible for sponsoring the process in the organization and also taking the ownership for steering it through the maze that any nascent organizational initiative would have to navigate. It is here that the HR set-up in the organization can play a significantly positive and constructive role.

In saying HR, it is implied that they are represented by the entire team of HR professionals, irrespective of their current function, sphere of responsibility and the nature of work they are currently engaged in. Not just training, learning and development professions, on whom perhaps falls the primary ownership, but also the head and different functionaries who fall within the ambit of being called HR.

So what can they do to facilitate an easy and trouble-free introduction of the initiative into the employee development process? What can the HR do to help Executive Coaching integrate and gain acceptance in the organization system? And, what role can the HR play to create a favourable and conducive ambience for Executive Coaching in the organization? There are steps that the HR can take to work out a good move forward in the process. These work to ease the process into the organization and, in a sense, make the organization Executive Coaching–friendly.

PRE-EMPT AND PROJECT COMPETENCY AND SKILL NEEDS

Talent management is today big business and the cornerstone of HR activity in organizations. Not just the hiring function of sourcing and acquiring talent for the organization, but also projecting for changes in the talent landscape industry-wide and within the organization. The HR has the responsibility to pre-empt the requirements of the organization in the periods to come and also prepare the strategy for approaching the requirements.

Having said this, retention and development of the existing talent is also the immediate concern of the HR. This calls for inventory of the existing talent pool, computing the gaps and deficiencies and looking at the possible upgradation of competency and skills of the existing pool within the organization.

Pricing the talent is a critical function that the HR has to undertake. The high-value talent has to be nurtured and constantly tended to through interventions such as Executive Coaching to not only keep them at the forefront of the talent scale, but also provide them overt indications of how the organization values them.

Among the menu of learning and development interventions available to the HR to work out the constant-renewal model for the high-value talent is Executive Coaching as a top-draw choice. All too often, the HR function has the difficulty in estimating the worth of the intervention itself, devoid of personal exposure and experience of it and also the inherent scepticism in investing so highly in people who they may not wholly believe in investing in.

Moving from being an uninvolved, inert administrative catalyst, crunching numbers to fill people positions, HR needs to walk into an image makeover with hands-on involvement in the competency, skill, personality and overall development of the individuals within. The ability of Executive Coaching to deliver value-upgrade with a personal touch is a great L&D initiative that HR can invest in.

DECIDE ON EXECUTIVE COACHING AS THE CHOSEN L&D METHODOLOGY

It is the L&D professionals within HR who have to work out the rationale and necessity for Executive Coaching being used as the method of choice for a particular L&D objective. The L&D professionals have to weigh their options against that of the other adult learning and employee development strategies available for the necessary growth and development of the chosen group of high-value people assets.

The weighing and deciding process needs information and consideration of some important factors such as the output objective, the value of the people asset in consideration, the felt need to upgrade the competencies and capabilities, the relative time available for the intervention, the willingness of the individuals to be involved and invest in the process, availability of the appropriate executive coach, the budget allocation available and its adequacy, the buy-in of other stakeholders, etc. Taking all these into consideration, the decision on whether Executive Coaching is the intervention of choice or should it be one of the more traditional methodologies can be made.

This too is within the realm of HR responsibility because in the end, HR will have to sell the idea in the first place and be accountable for it in the later stages, whatever the outcome.

Caselet 10 **Taste the Medicine You Prescribe**

"Ten years ago, I sat there too," said Ananth Kasbekar pointing to the chair in the far corner. "The same meeting room. Except, then it did not have the honourable name it has today. I was also just as skeptical when my boss, Arojit Chakraborthy, at that time the Vice-President (HR), was speaking about the 'great'," Kasbekar paused as he lifted both hands up, symbolically drawing quotation marks in the air with his fingers, "benefits he had got from Executive Coaching," he continued.

Kasbekar was addressing the Quarterly HR Meeting in the company. He was the Vice President and Head of HR in the company now. The theme of this meeting was L&D Initiatives in the company. And Kasbekar was speaking of his exposure and experience with Executive Coaching.

"I had gone back from the meeting wondering who will bell the cat and tell the VP(HR) that he should stop wasting so much good money on these fancy Executive Coaching things and get down to basic classroom training. Somehow Arojit got to know what I was thinking. And a few months later, he called me to his office and told me to consider meeting the executive coach who was working with the CEO and senior executives then. He gave me some feedback on areas I should consider focusing on, and told me to work out an appointment with the coach.

"I did that the following week and reluctantly met the coach. There was something in the way the initial session went that, somehow, I found myself drawn to sessions after session till I was so taken in by the transformation and change I could see in myself. I started becoming more confident about myself and my work. I was able to notice even small and minute things that made a big difference in the way I looked at issues and problems with people and our systems. The way I interacted with people—in the office and my friends too ... there was a new depth in my understanding and personality. I also found myself being appreciated more. Even my family had noticed the changes in my outlook and personality.

"The sessions were not tough or demanding in anyway, but the insights and the clarity were such that the change was so easy. I spent few months with the executive coach and then we moved on. But those sessions have been the turning point of my life. From then on, I have been perhaps the most vocal fan of the process and have recommended so many senior colleagues to it. They too have in turn suggested it to others.

"What I am telling you is that as HR professionals, we must have the faith in the L&D interventions that have been tried and tested. And more importantly, we should have the openness to go through and experience them ourselves. That will give us the best taste and flavor of what we are suggesting to others. I have learnt the lesson taking the long road. You don't have to. Be open and we will be able to convince others to adopt change for the better through L&D interventions."

BELIEVE IN EXECUTIVE COACHING

For in any way the culture and practice of Executive Coaching to take root, HR itself believing in it is at the head of the list of essentials. Human Resource department is the primary process-owner and being essentially the parent of the process within the organization, their belief in the system and intervention not only colours the image of the intervention, but also contributes heavily to the success of the planning, design and execution the Executive Coaching intervention.

The conviction with which the process is introduced, explained and sold to the potential coaches would ride heavily on the belief invested in the process by the custodians and administrators of the scheme. Human Resource department's faith in the system soaks into the very fabric of the process within the organization, influencing how others take to the system and the process as they enter it.

The credibility of the Executive Coaching rests on how HR is able to project, drive and gain popular support. Being convinced of its efficacy will make a huge difference in building faith in the process. 'Selling' the intervention to the rest of the organization becomes easy when belief in the process is high.

GETTING TOP TEAM BUY-IN

Critical to the success of the process is the ability of the HR to get the top team of the organization on board before the launch of the scheme. This depends largely on the relationship that HR has with the top team and their perception of the ability and capability of HR to steer the scheme through the organization.

Being so, HR has to work at preparing the brief that will be presented to the top team, the issues, the justifications, the accrued advantages, backgrounders relating to the people being targeted, the cost, time duration and design of the intervention, etc. The intervention may not get adapted by mere documentation of the projected benefits on paper, and would, all too often, require personal selling by the HR. Unless the top team themselves are familiar with the process and have experienced it themselves, some persuasion may often be needed—and in some cases, aggressive selling.

In most organizations, it is the writ of the top team that runs. Even in the most democratized of set-ups, the opinion and persuasions of the top team is what gets the wheels turning to get the cart moving forward. Rather than struggle to get the top team on board, if the intervention flounders or gets stalled, it would certainly be a good option to take to get the top team's alignment and agreement with the process before its introduction in the organization.

At the end of the day, the best thing that will eventually be going in favour of the Executive Coaching culture and intervention in the organization is the top team buy-in. It will be well worth the initial investment. The payoffs would accrue pretty much later on.

IDENTIFYING THE HIGH-POTENTIAL PEOPLE ALONG WITH THE TOP TEAM

While the organization has an array of employee development strategies to choose from, the investment into high-potential and high-value individuals has to be distinct. Distinct in that it has to deliver a higher quality and higher value results. Then again, the opportunity to individualize the development opportunity and offering is invaluable in designing a distinct development intervention for those expected to be in the forefronts of the organizational leadership and work in the future.

To this end, the ability of HR to identify these individuals and customize development efforts to their specific needs and ability makes Executive Coaching an option of choice. Therefore comes the role of HR in working with the top team in identifying these high-worth and high-potential people within the organization.

HR has to work towards having a concerted strategy and scheme to identify these people from within, while also keeping in mind that a positive discrimination such as this could result in avoidable ill-will and unrest amongst the organizational community. At the worst, it could vitiate organizational culture if not handled well and tactfully. It is here that the buy-in of the top team could also come in handy.

Each organization and its top team have their own view and perspective on who the high potential and high value people are. Also, the individualized learning as a strategy is something that the top team should ideally have experienced themselves. And having benefited from it, would like to extend it to the valued people in the organization.

ASSESSING AND DETERMINING LEARNING AND DEVELOPMENT NEEDS

Learning and development needs-assessment is an essential part of the HR function. The issue has much to do with the priority accorded to the L&D activity and function in the scheme of things for the HR. The priority accorded often reflects in the accuracy and the utility of the exercise to the organization. Particularly, in the case of the intended Executive Coaching efforts, the nature of the intervention itself lends to requiring a higher level if importance being given to the assessment. The assessment is important at the start of the intervention itself.

There are different methods and approaches to determine the L&D needs of people in the organization. Of particular interest would be the ones that connect the career planning process with the L&D projection. This would provide valuable data to help with the initial approaches in the Executive Coaching intervention. HR familiarity with the L&D requirement of the individuals being introduced to the Executive Coaching process would be valuable in administering and eventually working out an effectiveness evaluation process.

Career planning and growth information along with the specific L&D needs data will be an invaluable input into increasing the value of the Executive Coaching effort and output. This would help the coach focus better the approach, design and activities within the process to the needs of the coachee.

SELLING THE EXECUTIVE COACHING PROCESS TO THE PROSPECTIVE COACHEES

HR's role in selling the idea is critical. Being the process owner in the organization, a convincing statement and pitch from the HR would go a long way in the faith that the prospective coachees have in the Executive Coaching process. Preparing the ground for the introduction of the process is as critical a role that HR needs to play as any other during the process.

To generate interest in the process, HR should take it on themselves to provide as much information and data as possible to help the entrants in the process to understand better and approach the entry in to the system easier. As much as providing the information, importance lies in also generating interest in the intervention. Towards this end, enlisting the past beneficiaries of the intervention within and, in some cases, outside the organization is a good idea to bolster the image of the intervention. Direct interaction, where it is possible, would be of great value.

Meeting the prospective participants in the intervention prior to the start or announcement of the intervention would be a positive step in the direction. To some extent, handholding the system till the introduction of the coaches and the contact between them and the coaches would still be within the domain of the HR role. HR could even leverage their personal equations and relationships with the senior executive proposed to be provided the Executive Coaching opportunity.

Often, the coachees, not knowing what they are being led into, would like the endorsement from someone they look up to or are familiar with. This would be seen as a reassuring thing. For the new entrant, HR is always familiar and a word from them helps in a big way. In other cases, those unconvinced with the Executive Coaching process or the need for it for them would need quite some effort and work put in to get them to accept and come in.

SOURCE HIGH-CALIBRE COACHES

Coaching intervention can only be as good as the coaches who are invited to participate and take on the responsibility. Sourcing high-calibre coaches is the innate responsibility of the HR set-up. This means HR cannot expect to start off on the introduction of the intervention without sufficient groundwork and long time spent on the network to get the best possible coaches into the organizational ambit.

It would be good for HR to build, over time, a network of contact with experienced and high-calibre coaches who may specialize in different field, different areas of expertise and different approaches. This would give HR a menu to choose from, depending on the current requirements.

Another approach is to have someone the organization has been working with, is familiar with it and is excellent—having done well with other people in the organization—on a retainer for the organization. This coach could be available when called on; the advantage here being the comfort the organization, HR and the people have with the resource and leveraging the accumulated knowledge and wisdom of the coach with respect to the organization.

FACILITATE CREATING THE RIGHT AMBIENCE

HR being the effectual custodian of the organization culture also bears the responsibility in creating the kind of ambience needed for the introduction of any positive intervention. The Executive Coaching intervention to be successful requires the building up of, maintaining and nurturing an environment conducive for the sustenance of the relationship and practice. The need is to work out with the coach the kind of environment most suited for the intervention and working on strategy to create and hold the environment.

This requires the HR to understand very well the dynamic of the environment that is endemic to the organization. Keeping this in mind, the effort is to tweak it towards the required one, especially with respect to the ones surrounding those involved in the intervention. HR may need to intervene actively in areas that tend to influence negatively the context and the situation in which the Executive Coaching practice is being carried out. The relationship and the effort is very much sensitive to the intervention of several environmental factors such as the opinion of the people at the peer level; the attitude of the superiors and other stake holders; the image of Executive Coaching itself in the organization; etc.

HR has to not only create and provide the right environment at the beginning of the intervention itself, but also monitor the changes and health of the environment in relation to the Executive Coaching throughout. This being the ideal state, anything approaching this lends substantially to the success of the intervention.

Further, in the initial stages, particularly when the invited coach is external and not yet well-versed with the ways and contours of the organizational culture, the HR has to facilitate the maintenance of the appropriate environment. Even when the executive coach is internal and is well-versed in the ways of the culture within, HR may still need to be on alert to prevent any form of negative influences from creeping in. This effectual culture sentry role is crucial till the intervention and practice takes firm root. Then on, the Executive Coaching practice and relationships would be quite resilient.

BRIEF EXECUTIVE COACHES

This is a sensitive role that HR would find itself in. On one hand, coaches are chary of any form of interference in the process; they would also expect a level of information and brief from the 'host' of the process. Further, the coachees would not be in favour of any brief about them from the organization, or for that matter from the HR about themselves. This may, if not handled well, affect the credibility and progress in the Executive Coaching process. Therefore, this has to be handled delicately without offending or falling foul of anyone else in the system.

It could also turn out to be a delicate balancing act when there are motivated people in the top team with some form of agenda or interest in some of the people being introduced into the Executive Coaching process. They would often ask or, in some other form, pressurize HR into slipping some brief to the coach before the start of the process. They may, at times, also pull rank and ask to speak directly to the executive coach.

It would be to the advantage of the HR to have an understanding, tolerant and, perhaps, flexible executive coach. If the executive coach is familiar with the ways of the organization, he would be able to navigate past these. Otherwise, it would do well for the HR to take any of the following options.

HR could be open and speak with the executive coach upfront and brief him about the organization's approach to the process and leave it to the executive coach to figure out how he intends to take the brief and to what extent he intends to use or go by the brief. On the other hand, HR could choose to come in with the brief after the initial introduction and contact session between the executive coach and the coachee has taken place. This may help the executive coach put the brief in a context and see it in the right perspective.

HR could also take it on themselves to let the executive coach know that the member of the top team has expressed a need to speak with the executive coach to find out about the process and also brief about the coachee from his team. While most seasoned executive coaches would like this approach and also speak with the senior executive, some may prefer to buy time and speak after the start of the sessions.

The approach sometimes adopted by HR, although not recommended, is to be furtive about the brief and try to slip it in during informal conversations with the executive coach. While the HR could feel good for having sneaked in the brief, the smart executive coach would have figured out the motive in such an act. Such activities repeated often could turn out to be an irritant and adversely affect the relationship between the executive coach and the HR. This approach is best avoided.

Caselet 11 A Wish Is No Command

Three text messages and four missed calls could only mean one thing—something was on fire! So I called back immediately.

"Sir, I have been trying to get in touch with you urgently," was the frantic beginning without even a "hello" from Madhu Sinha, the young Assistant Manager, HRD. "Sir, we will have to postpone the Kick-off session for tomorrow. Acharya Sir has said it must be postponed. I don't know what to do. We have made all the arrangements and have invited all the senior people too." She said all this almost in one breath.

It took her a few minutes to regain her composure and calm herself enough to convey that Srinivasa Acharya, the Senior Vice President in charge of the North America Business based out of New Jersey, had asked to speak with the executive coach before the India Head in his Business Unit, Glen Roberts, gets into the coaching intervention. To Madhu Sinha, when Srinivasa Acharya says "before", it could mean that the entire session involving around 20 other senior people will have to be put off if Acharya's "request" is not taken care of. This becomes particularly difficult for Madhu Sinha when her head of department is away from office for an extended period. Srinivasa Acharya does not have to pull rank. He just has that kind of effect on people.

"Sir, can you please call Acharya sir and talk to him. We will have to somehow convince him to let Glen Sir join the coaching programme," Madhu Sinha almost pleaded. "Sure, Madhu, I'll speak with Mr Acharya today," I assured Madhu Sinha, "Please go ahead with the arrangements for the session tomorrow."

Srinivasa Acharya had a calm, measured and clear speech that somehow did not match the image people had built of him in the India Office. "Thank you for calling, Professor. I hope I did not upset any of your plans. I just wanted to have a word with you to let you know how important Glen is to our operations here at the North America Business. He is the most critical person supporting us from India. We have a lot riding on him and expect him to do great things for us.

"I am glad he is going to be with you. I also wanted to assure you of any help or feedback you may need from me any time in the process. I know I don't have any active role in the coaching but I would like you to know that I am one hundred percent with Glen and you," Srinivasa Acharya continued.

Srinivasa Acharya had no intension of interfering with the intervention. He just wanted to be heard when his critical resource was involved. The top team often would like to be involved in just being there for any help if needed. While the senior people in HR have the maturity to understand this, the younger people need to learn it soon enough.

HELP CHOOSE COACHING APPROACH

The choice of coaching approach is the prerogative of the executive coach. He would base his decision on several considerations and may have his own preferred style. Even so, the HR could help in understanding the normal L&D approach found to be effective, any data on learning styles of coachees and the prevalent organization culture. This would go a long way in helping the coach make up his mind in the choice of the approach.

Here again, it would be prudent to exercise caution in not exceeding in enthusiasm and pushing the limits of involvement of the HR in the process of coaching. It will also be good to remember that what may have worked well in one circumstance may not work all too well in others. Steer clear of temptation to participate in the process and leave the decision to the executive coach.

COORDINATION AND FACILITATION/LOGISTICAL SUPPORT

The feeling of satisfaction in the process is strongly dependent on the smooth progress in it. For smooth progression in the Executive Coaching, administrative support in the form of facilitation, coordination and logistical support will be required. The facilitation is in the event of needing organizational resources that could be made available to the executive coach or the coachee to take appropriate steps in the L&D path. This could also require meeting with other executives in the organization, or even exposure to different processes that may aid in the growth of experience and practice of the coachee.

The simple logistical support of meeting arena, space and privacy for the conduct of contact sessions, stationery, secretarial support, etc., adds to the feeling of the system working well. Even if it is only the coordination of arranging meetings or acquiring resource requirements, it would still be a good and favourable addition.

Being the administrator and facilitator also has its own advantages and benefits that accrue in favour of the HR and HR practices within the organization. Having a one-point contact for the intervention would work better when the number of activities within the Executive Coaching intervention are too many and diverse.

TRACK PROGRESS/REVIEW AND EVALUATION

HR has the responsibility to continually monitor the progress of the Executive Coaching process informally, more as a pre-emptive effort to head off any possible bottleneck and barriers that may inadvertently crop up. Also, it serves as an opportunity to keep tabs on the health of the intervention itself. Without being intrusive, HR needs to have an idea of the progress and the relative comfort of the participants and the executive coach as well.

Being a high-value and high-investment effort, the continual good tidings from the activity bodes well. The top team would also like an informal brief on how the effort is progressing. And then the executive coach and the coachee may also use HR as a sounding board. For this purpose, HR being knowledgeable is bound to be a contributory advantage.

In some organizations, there would be a need for formal evaluation of the outcome of the intervention. While the evaluation and feedback from the intervention has to be handled a whole lot differently from the conventional L&D processes, an indicative evaluation and feedback mechanism introduced in the process would not be considered out of place and may be taken well. Helping organize what can be introduced and carried out to meet the necessity, and satisfaction of all connected with the process, is of importance. Particularly the stakeholders like the top team, the finance and audit department, the departments from where the coachees come, etc., would require some form of evaluation of the process when completed or when nearing completion.

It is here that the HR can play a facilitative function. Different stakeholders would ask for different forms of evaluative feedback and the process being unlike the conventional training and development interventions, structured and specifically directed feedback may not always be possible or may run contrary to the opinions of the executive coach or the coachees. Navigating through this is a delicate work for the HR.

A good approach would be to prepare the ground for the use or otherwise of any post-intervention evaluation. Before the commencement itself, letting the stakeholders know about the nature and possibility of feedback would be good. This may help pre-empt and run-off any unexpected and unreasonable demands.

INPUT TO TOP TEAM ON MOVEMENT IN EMPLOYEE LEARNING

The fact that the top team has decided to invest in the employee and offer him an opportunity in the Executive Coaching initiative means the individual is important and is of high value to the organization in the scheme of things as seen by them. This would lead naturally to the top team wanting to be kept abreast of the developments in the individual's progress and the difference the L&D initiative is bringing in. The top team would almost expect the HR to brief them periodically on the status of the initiative and the movement that has been made.

Not always is this a possible activity and there is always the issue of ethics and the willingness of the coach to share or even report progress, but the expectation on the HR is even then a burden of the yoke that needs to be borne. Tact and delicate handling is called for and that would help HR avoid many a slip and unnecessary discomfort or even damage the image of the process.

EVALUATE AND REVIEW INTERVENTION

While the Executive Coaching process has peculiarity of its own with regard to evaluation itself and the worth of continuation of the intervention, the issue of evaluation of the process is often raised. This brings on to the HR the need to take a stand, hold on to the commitment to the process. HR should, to the very last, not allow the process to be skewed to meet the procedure-adherence need of people less informed about it. While this would be best explained and tackled at the start of the intervention, it is nevertheless essential to have the stand reiterated periodically so as not to cause any disruption of the intervention once it is underway.

Even if in some form evaluation of the process is being undertaken, the clarity with regard to it among all the stakeholders is the responsibility of the HR. Whether it is the process that is being evaluated or the outcome, or the progress made by the people, the clarity and design of the evaluation process is nevertheless that of HR.

HR must, in this case, take care and heed the advice of those whose help is being taken to design the evaluation process and the instruments being used. While most often the preferred approach would be subjective and indicative, the administration and the parameters should be meticulously taken care of by HR.

POST-COACHING INTEGRATION (PLANNING, PREPARATION AND DEPLOYMENT)

Executive Coaching has a purpose, which is to make an investment in the coachee and make progress so as to make him better in the respects set out. Being this, it is also necessary to follow up after the Executive Coaching intervention to ensure that the individual is placed and deployed in a position that best leverages the advantages of having undergone the L&D intervention.

It is, therefore, the responsibility of HR to undertake this activity as well. Planning for the proper integration of the individual after going through the Executive Coaching is as important. HR must work with the top team in planning well ahead the strategy for the immediate and the intermediate future of the individual post–Executive Coaching.

The pitfalls in not taking care of this is very real and unnecessarily expensive. Raised aspirations come with enhanced capabilities and competencies along with heightened awareness of one's worth. This increases the chances of the individual chaffing with the system that do not respond to nor accommodate the need to exercise the increased capability. HR must recognize this at the outset and move to address the issue.

Briefing the top team and working within the organizational system, HR must plan to relook at the role, responsibility and adequate leveraging of the individual. When this is not addressed and with closing of possible avenues of expressing higher capabilities, the advantages that accrue from the Executive Coaching intervention may well be lost with time. This is best averted when HR is proactive.

So long as the HR is convinced of the efficacy and need for the intervention, the chances of it succeeding increases dramatically. After all, HR is the responsible hub of almost all organizational-culture-related L&D interventions in the organization.

It would be good to have an aware and enlightened organizational culture. An ambience that is receptive and executive coach–friendly would make the intervention more fruitful and productive. And then, the most crucial organizational pivot around which the success of Executive Coaching can be built is HR. Their role is certainly important in the scheme of things in the organization.

10. FAQs ON EXECUTIVE COACHING

1. Where do we get executive coaches?
2. Can we do without executive coaches?
3. What's the difference between executive coaching and other forms of coaching?
4. How is an executive coach different from a mentor?
5. Can the executive coach really solve my problems?
6. Will the executive coach help with personal problems?
7. How does an organizational coach differ from a personal coach?
8. Do I need to tell my executive coach everything?
9. Can I trust my executive coach with all the information I share with him?
10. How long does the executive coaching last?
11. How long does each session generally last?
12. How frequently should I meet the executive coach in contact sessions?
13. Is there a certification or accreditation needed for executive coaches?
14. Can I become an executive coach?

1. Where do we get executive coaches?

Executive coaches are professionals. They belong to a niche occupied by those among L&D professionals who have a specialization in working with people on a one-on-one basis for their individual development in the identified areas. While there are executive coaches who specialize in overall development of the coachee, others work in areas they have a specialty and competence in.

Executive coaches do not normally advertise themselves but do go by references and endorsements of their work with others who have accessed and benefited from their association with the coach. Good coaches are known by the work they have done and the quality of people they have coached.

There are also associations and consortia formed by coaches in different geographies. These can be googled and contacted through their websites and other identifiers.

2. Can we do without executive coaches?

The answer is obviously 'yes'. One can choose to work his own way along the path of life, career or the organizational hierarchy. The L&D need of the individual can be sourced on their own and also be a part of any organizational initiative that works with groups participating in the initiatives. But one can definitely lead a life less ordinary by associating with a coach too. The individual attention that the executive coach can provide in development helps customize the L&D to the individual requirement.

There is a good stretch between being ordinary and exceptional. And then, even the good ones prefer to work towards becoming the best. They take on the services of an executive coach to make the difference between being pedestrian and being the best. The call is really left to the individual.

3. What's the difference between Executive Coaching and other forms of coaching?

The executive coach is one working on a one-on-one basis in helping senior and top executives in organizations with their L&D initiatives. Generally, Executive Coaching is a high-value initiative offered to critical and prized people resources at the higher levels of management. These executives have special needs considering they have lesser time and higher commitments with high stakes and investments riding on them. The executive coach covers a wide range of the L&D needs of the coachees. He has a wider repertoire of capabilities, tools and competencies he can call upon. Executive coaches normally work with individuals and seldom with groups.

On the other hand, other forms of coaching may focus on specific aspects of the needs of people in the organization. They may have a narrow focus of specific skill or performance area being addressed. They may also work with groups of people at the same time. The skill required here varies with the approach and the context.

4. How is an executive coach different from a mentor?

Both the executive coach and the mentor have a close association with the coachee and the mentee, respectively. They have the best interests of the coachee and the mentee at heart. The major focus of both is to enhance the effectiveness and success of their wards in performance and career.

Having said these, there however exist distinct differences between the nature, practice and the duration of association of the executive coach with the coachee and the mentor with the mentee. The relationship between them also is different as a consequence.

The executive coach and the coachee have an association which is clearly driven by objective and purpose. The association between them is built around this. Therefore, the nature of interactions and the scheduling of the interactions have a strong specific professional purpose and are less emotive. On the other hand, the association between the mentor and the mentee has a larger purpose of the overall development of the mentee in aspects not limited to the professional life and performance. The mentor has an inspirational presence in the mentee's mind and life, while the executive coach has a professional role-based presence.

Then again, the work and the activities involved in the Executive Coaching involvement are much more structured and scheduled around achieving tangible time-bound objectives. The mentoring association is far more loosely structured and therefore the scheduling of the interactions is also informal. To this extent, the relationship between the executive coach and the coachee tends to be more formal than that between the mentor and his mentee.

The mentoring relationship is built over a length of time and is mutually accepted over a clearly understood but not necessarily formalized protocol. The coaching relationship on the other hand has a distinct protocol and rules of engagement. The mentoring relationship is not bound by an outside limit of time and can continue over a lifetime. The Executive Coaching relationship and association is over a specified period of time and has a clear point of end to it.

There is no personal gain that the mentor is looking for in the mentoring relationship. He is in it for only the gratification derived out of seeing the mentee succeed. The executive coach is a professional and, unlike the mentor, is normally compensated for his work. Mentors tend to be wise and removed from the competitive aspect of life or work, but the executive coach is very much cued into competitiveness.

5. Can the executive coach really solve my problems?

Guaranteeing that the problems can be solved is certainly a matter of prophesy without knowing anything about the problem itself. Therefore, whether in Executive Coaching or in any other profession that works with a measure of problem solving as a mandate, such guarantees are at best difficult to offer. However, on whether the executive coach can solve problems, it must be said that it is among the items on top of the list of work he is good at. Further, the executive coach really does not solve the problem, but helps the coachee solve it himself in the true sense.

The nature of the problem, the extent to which the coachee is willing to work at solving the problem, the time frame available and other environmental factors dictate whether the problem will be solved or otherwise. The dynamics between the coachee and the executive coach also influence the approach to the problem itself. Eventually, it really depends on the coachee on how the problem will be approached, worked at and solved in the end. The executive coach is really the facilitator in the process.

6. Will the executive coach help with personal problems?

The realm of the executive coach is built around the professional work and performance of the coachee. However, particularly in the Indian context, it is not possible to contain professional life within the bounds of office time. There is a significant leak of expectations, mores and behaviours born in the familial settings into the workplace. So, also the intertwining of the personal life of the individual with his work-life entails that the executive coach must address the issues in personal life while working with the professional side of the coachee.

However, some coaches prefer to refer the coachee to a counsellor or similar expert in matters relating to the personal side of the coachee's life. Particularly when the executive coach finds the personal issues convoluted and he is not able to work with or devote sufficient time, or is out of his depth, he may prefer to refer the coachee to someone else. Most coaches, at the same time, also help the coachees resolve and deal with issues in the personal space as well. In the Indian context, this is seen as a normal practice, but in other cultures, personal life is kept separate from work-life.

So, the executive coach could help work with personal problems as well. It would be good to check this out before building an association with the coach and also understanding his individual views on this.

7. How does an organizational coach differ from a personal coach?

For one, the organizational coach is selected and contracted to work on the intervention by the organization, and the personal coach is on a direct personal contract with the individual. To this extent, who pays the coach for his work is the difference.

The other differences manifest themselves out of this. The organizational coach, being contracted through the organization, has to bear in mind the organizational dynamics as well. They will have the HR department as one of the parties to interface with in the intervention process. There is also the view of the senior management that he needs to keep in mind and choose how he needs to deal with them. Then again, while the primary concern of the executive coach is the growth and development of the coachee, there may also be other intervening organizational factors to be balanced.

The personal coach is under no obligation to consider the factors that exist within the organization. He may choose to heed them to extent of their impacting the interests of the coachee. His concern is the dynamics of the relationship with the coachee, having contracted to work with the coachee who is also the subject of the contract.

At the same time, there may exist advantages on both sides as well. The organizational coach has access to the resources of the organization, such as literature and knowledge, the experienced pool of people in the organization, infrastructure and facilitation, etc. The personal coach has also the freedom to chart courses that he may not have the liberty to otherwise.

8. Do I need to tell my executive coach everything?

While it would be good to get an answer to this in 'Yes' or 'No', it would not be right to give either. It is akin to the way one would treat going to the medical doctor. Does one need to tell the doctor everything? Maybe not. But, ideally, one should let the good doctor know everything so that he can make an informed diagnosis and a better quality decision. So also it is with the executive coach.

There is no norm or rule about everything being shared. And the executive coach himself will offer you the choice of not sharing something you may not want to. But believing in the executive coach and establishing a relationship built on trust can help in taking the call on sharing everything with the executive coach a little easier.

There is also the issue of what the 'everything' covers. The executive coach is primarily concerned with the professional development and growth of the individual. Therefore, his concern will be with any aspect that has a bearing on this side of the individual. So, 'everything' can be taken as all those aspects that has a connection with the professional side. In this case, the 'everything' that may fall in the 'everything else' category is a matter of choice. The ideal would be to take the 'everything' and 'everything else' as one combined lot.

The reason why it is important to share as much as you can with the executive coach is to help him get a holistic picture of you as a person. He would certainly be better placed to figure out what is in your best interest. If the concern, however, is of confidentiality, then it would be best addressed at the very beginning of the association before the need for such a call comes up.

9. Can I trust my executive coach with all the information I share with him?

Trust and confidentiality are the cornerstones of the Executive Coaching process. Every executive coach knows well that the key to establishing a successful functional relationship depends much on the faith the coachee has in the coach not only in terms of his capability and competence, but also in his adherence to the ethical values of the Executive Coaching practice. The fundamental ethical value here is confidentiality.

The Executive Coaching process addresses this particular aspect at the very outset itself. The executive coach clarifies this issue at the introductory session, and also later when the protocols and expectations are being discussed. The clarity on the ethical bindings on confidentiality and non-exploitative nature of the relationship is assured and agreed upon early on in the process.

At the same time, it would also be good for the coachee to seek any form of assurances from those he may trust. This may be in checking the references of the executive coach and the experiences of people earlier with the coach. In the organizational context, the HR would be a good source of ensuring the credence of the executive coach before entering into the intervention.

At the same time, it must be kept in mind that the ethical values and practices are self regulated and not affirmed by any monitoring authority in Executive Coaching practice. The executive coach is bound by the values he espouses, and his practice and reputation is established by the credibility he has garnered. Therefore, the due diligence done by the coachee or someone on his behalf will be well in place.

Therefore, you can trust the executive coach with the information you share with him. Do establish a trusting relationship first.

10. How long does the Executive Coaching last?

Executive Coaching does not have a standard one-size-fits-all routine. The entire exercise is customized to the requirements of the individual coachee. The coach adapts the approach, process and the routine to the L&D needs of the coachee.

The duration of the Executive Coaching depends on how long it takes for the executive coach and the coachee to satisfactorily complete and achieve the objectives they have set for themselves. The objectives would include the development targets and the resolution of the issues facing the coachee.

The normal period of engagement of the process would range from a few weeks to several months. Then again, the contractual engagement of the intervention could also determine the duration of the Executive Coaching process. For instance, if the organizational contract is for a specific number of engagements or a specified period, then the coach and the coachee will have to work within the allocated time and session parameters. But usually the executive coaches prefer to leave the time frame and number of sessions open with a contract for the entire intervention.

11. How long does each session generally last?

The contact sessions in the Executive Coaching process are usually scheduled by mutual consent. The sessions generally last between one and two hours. Sometimes, if there are more extensive discussions, inventories or experimental activities, the sessions may be extended further as may be necessary.

Each session typically begins with the recap of the previous work to put the current session in a context and build a suitable environment for the session. Then it progresses into the activity or discussion scheduled for the current session. This takes most of the time in the session. On completion of the activity, the executive coach takes stock of the progress in the process so far before looking at the work needed to be done ahead. He would then work with the coachee to look at the work that needs to be done in the intersession period before the next session.

The coachee is normally invited to clarify or discuss any doubts or issues that he may have before concluding the session.

12. How frequently should I meet the executive coach in contact sessions?

The frequency of the contact sessions depends entirely on how the executive coach sees the progress in the intervention and his reading of the needs of the coachee. The sessions are generally arranged on mutual convenience.

The principle the executive coach works on is to try and keep the intervention active in the mind of the coachee. The executive coach generally designs the frequency around the convenience of the coachee as they are normally senior executives with a severe pressure for time. The coach keeps the frequency such that the coachee is influenced to work at a steady pace without the process slipping out of the mind and active thinking. To this end, the executive coach would insist that the contact sessions are schedules at least once every week to 10 days.

This frequency depends also on the push and priority the coachee gives to the effort. The coachee who is enthusiastic may like to speed up the process and work faster. This would mean more frequent sessions. If this is acceptable to the executive coach in terms of it fitting into the design and approach, then the frequency will be worked out accordingly.

Sometimes, the coachee may face certain sudden pressure of unexpected work schedule. In this case, the frequency is relaxed to accommodate the sudden spurt of work. However, the coach keeps in mind the extent to which the coachee continues to be involved in the process.

Then again, when there is some intense issue being worked upon or the resolution of some delicate matter being taken up, the executive coach may ask for sessions everyday. But these are more exceptions than the norm.

13. Is there a certification or accreditation needed for executive coaches?

There are several organizations that teach Executive Coaching and certify the learners to have become 'qualified' to practise Executive Coaching. There are also organizations that offer accreditation for a fee. Unlike medical, legal or accountancy professions, there are no certifying authorities—established or acting—whose consent is needed to practice Executive Coaching.

Teaching Executive Coaching is a tricky business. One can teach the skills and familiarize the learner with the issues that can be encountered in the field. But then a certificate of having attended a course or passed an examination would hardly be an acceptable replacement for wisdom, experience and the acumen to command the respect of senior executives in organizations. But the learning is a good start if the journey is followed through with years of dedicated work.

But certification and accreditation is quite another thing. The 'fee' charged is often the interest for the organizations offering the service and there is little told about the value of the accreditation or the standing of the organization offering it. Both these are an enticement to the gullible.

The Executive Coaching succeeds on the capability and reputation the executive coach has garnered over the years of practice. It would be good to work towards accruing this than chase after mirage of shortcuts.

14. Can I become an executive coach?

Anyone can do some form of coaching anytime. Coaching requires the ability to help someone acquire skill, capability or competence through a reasonably structured process of L&D. Coaching also implies that the learning is customized for the individual or a small group. This much can be worked by most people. But the issue is in sustaining this as a profession or over long periods of time consistently. Executive coach, on the other hand, is a higher level of being among coaches working in organizational settings.

The requirements for Executive Coaching are a different level of competency, skill, attitude and orientation. Executive Coaching generally deals with coaching executives at the senior and top levels of the organization. These are people with a high level of capability themselves. Hence, becoming a coach to these people requires matching them and exceeding their expectations in helping in their L&D. Executive Coaching also requires several additional skills and abilities. The requirement is also to be able to inspire confidence and build a coaching relationship with the coachees.

While it is perhaps possible to be involved in a coaching situation on a one-off basis, but to carry this on at a professional level requires years of training and work. It also calls for a width of experience and the wisdom to understand people and issues. All the same, we could all coach others in specific areas in which we have a high level of competence and also have the ability to coach. If we are short in something, we can always learn and take to helping others learn.

In a perfect world, we would all be coaches...

REFERENCES AND SUGGESTED READINGS

Argyris, C. and Schön, D., (1978) *Organizational Learning: A Theory of Action Perspective*. Reading, MA (USA): Addison Wesley.

Berglas, S., (2002) 'The Very Real Dangers of Executive Coaching', *Harvard Business Review*, 80(6): 86–92.

Beck, A. T., (1976) *Cognitive Therapy and the Emotional Disorders*. New York: New American Library.

Beck, J., (1995) *Cognitive Therapy: Basics and Beyond*. New York: Guilford Press.

Bernard, C. I., (1938) *The Functions of the Executive*. Cambridge, MA (USA): Harvard University Press.

Bion, W., (1962) *Learning from Experience*. London: Heinemann.

Bluckert,. P., (2010) 'The Gestalt Approach to Coaching'. In E. Cox, T. Bachkirova and D. Clutterbuck (eds), *The Complete Handbook of Coaching*, pp. 80–93. London: SAGE.

Brounstein, M., (2000) *Coaching and Mentoring for Dummies*. Foster City, CA (USA): IDG Books Worldwide.

Clutterbuck, D., (1998) *Learning Alliances: Tapping into Talent*. London: CIPD.

Clutterbuck, D. and Megginson, D., (2005) *Mentoring in Action: A Practical Guide for Managers*. London: Kogan Page.

Cox, E., Bachkirova, T. and Clutterbuck, D., (2010) *The Complete Handbook of Coaching*. London: SAGE.

Cox, E. and Jackson, P., (2010) 'Developmental Coaching'. In E. Cox, T. Bachkirova and D. Clutterbuck (eds), *The Complete Handbook of Coaching*, pp. 217–230. London: SAGE.

Ellis, A., Gordon, J., Neenan, M. and Palmer, S., (1997) *Stress Counseling: A Rational Emotive Behavior Approach*. New York: Springer.

Fitzgerald, C. and Berger, J. (eds), (2002) *Executive Coaching: Practices and Perspectives*. Palo Alto, CA (USA): Davies-Black Publishing.

Gallwey, T., (2000) *The Inner Game of Work: Overcoming Mental Obstacles for Maximum Performance*. London: Orion Business Books.

Goldsmith, M., Lyons, L. and Freas, A., (2000) *Coaching for Leadership: How the World's Greatest Coaches Help Leaders Learn*. San Francisco, CA (USA): Jossey-Bass.

Grant, A. M. and Cavanagh, M. J., (2010) 'Life Coaching'. In E. Cox, T. Bachkirova and D. Clutterbuck (eds), *The Complete Handbook of Coaching*, pp. 277–90. London: SAGE.

Greg, C., (1999) 'Someone To Look Up To', *Journal of Accountancy*, 188(5): 89–93.

Grimley, B., (2010) 'The NLP Approach to Coaching'. In E. Cox, T. Bachkirova and D. Clutterbuck (eds), *The Complete Handbook of Coaching*, pp. 187–200. London: SAGE.

Guptan, S. U., (1988) 'Paternalism in Indian Organizations', *ASCI Journal of Management*, 18(1): 77–86.

———, (2006) *Mentoring: A Practitioner's Guide to Touching Lives*. New Delhi: Response Books.

Handy, C., (1993) *Understanding Organizations*. Harmondsworth: Penguin.

Hawkins, P. and Smith, N., (2010) 'Transformational Coaching'. In E. Cox, T. Bachkirova and D. Clutterbuck (eds), *The Complete Handbook of Coaching*, pp. 231–44. London: SAGE.

Ibarra, H., (2000) 'Making Partner: A Mentor's Guide to the Psychological Journey', *Harvard Business Review*, March–April, 78(2): 146–55.

Jones, R. A., Rafferty and Griffin, M. A., (2006) 'The Executive Coaching Trend: Towards More Flexible Executive', *Leadership and Organisational Development Journal*, 27(7): 584–96.

Kampa-Kokesch, S. and Anderson, M., (2001) 'Executive Coaching: A Comprehensive Review of Literature', *Consulting Psychology Journal: Practice and Research*, 53(4): 205–28.

Kilberg, R. R., (2000) *Executive Coaching: Developing Managerial Wisdom in a World of Chaos*. Washington DC (USA): American Psychology Association.

Knowles, M., (1978), *The Adult Learner: A Neglected Species*. Houston, TX (USA): Gulf.

Knowles, M., Holton, E. and Swanson, R., (2005) *The Adult Learner*. Oxford: Elsevier Butterworth Heinemann.

Kolb, D., (1984) *Experiential Learning: Experience as a Source of Learning and Development*. Englewood Cliffs, NJ (USA): Prentice Hall.

Landsberg, M., (1997) *The Tao of Coaching*. London: Harper Collins.

Lee, G., (2003) *Leadership Coaching: From Personal Insights to Organizational Performance*. London: Chartered Institute of Personnel and Development.

———, (2010) 'The Psychodynamic Approach to Coaching'. In E. Cox, T. Bachkirova and D. Clutterbuck (eds), *The Complete Handbook of Coaching*, pp. 23–36. London: SAGE.

Levenson, H., (1998) 'Executive Coaching', *Consulting Psychology Review*, 48(2): 115–23.

Neenan, M. and Dryden, W., (2002) *Life Coaching: A Cognitive Behavioural Approach*. Hove: Routledge.

Newton, J., Long, S. and Sievers, B., (2006) *Coaching in Depth: The Organizational Role Consulting Approach*. London: Karnac Books.

Newton, T. and Napper, R., (2010) 'Transactional Analysis and Coaching'. In E. Cox, T. Bachkirova and D. Clutterbuck (eds), *The Complete Handbook of Coaching*, pp. 172–186. London: SAGE.

Orenstein, R., (2006) 'Measuring Executive Coaching Efficacy? The Answer was Right Here All Along', *Consulting Psychology Journal*, 58(2): 106–16.

———, (2007) *Multidimensional Executive Coaching*. New York: Springer.

Palmer, S., (2002) 'Cognitive and Organizational Models of Stress That are Suitable for Use within Workplace Stress Management/Prevention Coaching, Training and Counseling Settings', *The Rational Emotive Behavior Therapist*, 10(1): 15–21.

———, (2008) 'The PRACTICE Model of Coaching: Towards a Solution-focussed Approach', *Coaching Psychology International*, 1(1): 4–8.

Palmer, S., (2009) 'Rational Coaching: A Cognitive Behavioural Approach', *The Coaching Psychologist*, 5(10): 12–18.

Palmer, S. and Szymanska, K., (2007) '*Cognitive Behavioural Coaching: An Integrative Approach*'. In S. Palmer and A. Whybrow (eds), *Handbook of Coaching Psychology: A Guide for Practitioners*. Hove: Routledge.

Parsloe, E., (1992) *Coaching, Mentoring and Assessing: A Practical Guide to Developing Competence*. London: Kogan Page.

Parsloe, E. and Wray, M., (2000) *Coaching and Mentoring: Practical Methods to Improve Learning*. London : Kogan Page.

Peltier, B., (2001) *The Psychology of Executive Coaching: Theory and Application*. London: Brunner-Routledge.

Peterson, D., (1996) 'Executive Coaching at Work: The Art of One-on-one Change', *Consulting Psychology Journal*, 48(2): 78–86.

Reddin, W. J., (1970) *Managerial Effectiveness*. New York: McGraw Hill.

Reeves, R., (2001) *Happy Mondays: Putting the Pleasure Back into Work*. London: Momentum.

Rogers, C.R., (1959) 'A Theory of Therapy, Personality and Interpersonal Relationship as Developed in the Client-centered Framework.' In S. Koch (ed.), *Psychology: A Study of a Science. Vol. 3: Formulations of the Person and the Social Context*, pp. 184–256. New York: McGraw Hill.

Rowan. J., (1991) *Subpersonalities: The People Inside Us*. London: Routledge.

———, (2010) 'The Transpersonal Approach to Coaching'. In E. Cox, T. Bachkirova and D. Clutterbuck (eds), *The Complete Handbook of Coaching*, pp. 146–157. London: SAGE.

Starr, J., (2008) *The Coaching Manual: The Definitive Guide to the Process, Principles and Skills of Personal Coaching*. Harlow: Pearson Education Limited.

Stokes, J., (1994) 'Institutional Chaos and Personal Stress'. In A. Obholzer and V. Roberts (eds), *The Unconscious at Work*, pp. 121–128. London: Routledge.

Stokes, J. and Jolly, R., (2010) 'Executive and Leadership Coaching'. In E. Cox, T. Bachkirova and D. Clutterbuck (eds), *The Complete Handbook of Coaching*, pp. 121–128. London: SAGE.

Tichy, N., (2004) *The Leadership Engine: How Winning Companies Build Leaders at Every Level*. London: Collins Business.

Torbert, W., (1987) *Managing the Corporate Dream: Restructuring for Long Term Success*. Homewood, IL (USA): Dow Jones Irwin.

Virmani, B. R. and Guptan, S. U., (1991) *Indian Management*. New Delhi: Vision Books.

Watkin, M., (2003) *The First 90 Days*. Boston, MA (USA): Harvard Business School Press.

Williams, H., Edgerton, N. and Palmer S., (2010) 'Cognitive Behavioural Coaching'. In E. Cox, T. Bachkirova and D. Clutterbuck (eds), *The Complete Handbook of Coaching*, pp. 37–53. London: SAGE.

Winnicott, D., (1965) *The Maturational Process and the Facilitating Environment*. London: Penguin.

Zachary, L. J., (2005) *Creating a Mentoring Culture: The Organization's Guide*. San Francisco, CA (USA): Jossey-Bass.

Zaleznik, A., (1992) 'Managers and Leaders: Are They Different?', *Harvard Business Review*, April, 70(2): 126–36.

Zey, M., (1984) *The Mentor Connection*. Homewood, IL (USA): Dow Jones Irwin.

INDEX

ABOUT THE AUTHOR

SUNIL UNNY GUPTAN has been a mentor and executive coach to several CEOs and top executives in corporate and non-corporate organizations for the past two decades. He is also a popular speaker, trainer and consultant in India and other parts of the world, focusing on human relations, leadership development, communication, learning and employee development and other areas of people development.

As a popular trainer, his experience covers training chief ministers, cabinet ministers, top executives and officials in industry and government, trade union leaders and school teachers. His passion is in working with people and helping them help themselves.

Dr Guptan also teaches at the Indian Institute of Management Ahmedabad in the Communications area. He was Professor in the Human Resources area in the Administrative Staff College of India, Hyderabad for over a decade, and also Director at FORDE Consultants Pvt Ltd., Hyderabad.

Dr Guptan began his professional career as a journalist with the *Indian Express* before moving to Osmania University's Department of Communication and Journalism as a member of the faculty. He is now with Touching Lives, Hyderabad, founded to add value and make significant positive difference to the lives of people and communities.

He is the author of *Mentoring: A Practitioner's Guide to Touching Lives* (2006) and co-author of *Indian Management* (1991). He has published several articles in journals, monographs and popular publications. He has also written and produced several radio and educational television programmes.

Dr Guptan enjoys studying people, cultures, behaviours and societies. He invests his personal time in counselling and helping people repair and cope with strained relationships and troubled lives.

He can be contacted at mentor@touchinglives.co.in.